ENjoy!

Larry Guest (signature)

Sports Icons 'R Funny!

By LARRY GUEST

Published by Amazon Create Space

Cover design: Christa Hutchins, Kelley Vaughn-Kauffman

Larry Guest Books – P.O. Box 613 Cape Canaveral, FL 32920

Visit www.larryguest.com

Table of Contents

Introduction   4

Chapter 1 -- Bear Bryant   9

Chapter 2 – Mickey Mantle   25

Chapter 4 -- Payne Stewart, Ben Smith   43

Chapter 5 – Cris Collinsworth   56

Chapter 6 – Woody Hayes   62

Chapter 7 – Lou Holtz, Bobby Bowden   67

Chapter 8 – Joe Namath, Larry Grantham, Steve Sloan

Chapter 9 – Steve Spurrier, Peyton Manning   82

Chapter 10 – Don Shula   95

Chapter 11 – Walt Zembriski   102

Chapter 12 – Mike Shanahan, Charley Pell   110

Chapter 13 – Davey Johnson   117

Chapter 14 -- Arnold Palmer, Greg Norman   125

Chapter 15 – Hawk Harrelson   138

Chapter 16 – Bob Baffert, Ernie Els, Jimmy Johnson,
George Steinbrenner, Seve Ballesteros, Clint Hurdle
146

Introduction

AN ODD THING happens when a person is asked to recall the funniest things that happened during their career. The brain shuts down. Memory cells disengage. The person, for the life of him or her, can't recall a single hilarious moment, even though there may have been dozens.

In researching this book of little-known funnies involving sports icons I covered in my thirty-plus years as a sports columnist, I encountered that syndrome over and over. I already had a couple dozen anecdotes in mind in which I was directly involved, observed, or knew about. But each anecdote was about one page of copy and it was not likely that any publisher was interested in producing a 20-page book.

So I contacted most of those icons – at least those still alive – and people around them. My aim was to add some additional funny anecdotes on each chosen athlete or coach to expand those one-page vignettes into short chapters. When I contacted them, that vacant phenomenon took over. Thankfully, after taking a few days to mull the question, most of them remembered some laughable and/or insightful stories that I could add to each personality.

I can certainly relate to the sudden memory loss. A few years ago, a national sports writer colleague, Gene Wojciechowski, put together a book on funny things that happened to veteran pressboxers. When he contacted me for a contribution, I went absolutely blank. A few days later, I began to think of several and was upset with myself that I failed to help a fellow scribe. I kept asking myself why couldn't I think of the time that such-and-such happened? Gene said he would get back to me to see if could think of an amusing anecdote, but he never did. Finally, I contacted him, but the book was already being printed. One particular incident stood out above the rest and I found it baffling that the following hadn't instantly come to mind when Gene first reached out. . . .

A few years after I went to work for the *Orlando Sentinel* in the mid-'70s, I received a call from the teaching tennis pro at the Disney World Contemporary Hotel. Sandy Schunck, who later married teaching golf pro John Redman, wanted to know if we had a photo on file of New York Yankees pitcher Steve Kline. She explained that "Kline" had become an occasional visitor to her tennis complex and, at his request, she introduced him to some other vacationing tennis amateurs to set up informal games.

But something didn't seem quite right.

When I found a couple of photos of Kline, she drove into town to the *Sentinel* offices to take a look. It only took a second as she gasped in shock. "This isn't him!" she exclaimed, referring to the guy she had introduced to several Disney visitors as Steve Kline and arranged tennis games for him. She explained that he typically called a day ahead when he was headed to Central Florida and she promised to alert me when he called again.

A week later, Sandy called and gave me the flight number for his arrival later that day. She added a description – tall, slender and typically carrying a backgammon board. I met the flight -- back when you could greet arrivals right at the gate. My plan was to "interview" him as if I thought he was actually Steve Kline and pen a jocular column about exposing this impersonator. I didn't realize at the time that his ploy as an ersatz major league pitcher was to impress and befriend wealthy tourists, plying them with "inside" baseball stories to gain their confidence, then steal their credit cards and blank checks once he was welcomed into their hotel suites. Having Sandy introduce him as the Yankees starting pitcher unwittingly gave him credibility that the victims didn't question.

When "Kline" deplaned (real name Steve Wacaser) the backgammon board gave him away immediately. I approached him and asked for a brief interview. He denied he was Kline and walked away. Two hours later, Sandy called from the Contemporary Hotel tennis center, saying the imposter was there, playing with a hotel guest. I corralled a Sentinel photographer, jumped in my car and rushed to the scene.

When I arrived and stepped out of the car next to the court, the funniest thing happened.

Wacaser promptly walked to us and said, "Let's not make a scene. I'll go with you quietly." He sat down in the front passenger seat of my car and closed the door. The photographer and I looked at one another, blinking in confusion, not knowing what to do. I was happy he was in tennis garb and thus could see he was not armed. Except for a tennis racquet.

It turns out that when I approached him in the airport, he thought I was the FBI agent who had been tracking him. We drove him out of Disney World and back into town. I placed a tape recorder on the seat between us and said, simply, "Tell me about it." During the 30-minute ride, Wacaser trotted out a detailed confession of his scams, including names and dates and even his act of stealing a valuable coin collection from a New York priest who had taken him in as an indigent waif.

I mentioned I had to make a stop at the *Sentinel* and pulled up to the security booth and had a staffer call the police, very briefly explaining that a notorious con man was sitting in my car. I stepped inside the building just long enough for the police to arrive and question Waycaser. They radioed Orlando Police Department headquarters and discovered there were arrest warrants out for him in several states. They took him into custody and, about two months later, was sentenced to several years in jail for impersonation and forgery.

The real Steve Kline, who was dogged by a series of advisories that someone was impersonating him, was thankful to hear that the culprit had finally been captured by a pseudo "FBI agent.

When he was released from jail, he called me and said he'd like to visit. Naturally, I declined. (Years later, in 2010, Wacaser was sentenced to 16 years in federal prison for robbing two Illinois banks.)

I can safely say that during my 30-plus years as a columnist I was occasionally compared to certain unmentionable body parts and accused of being communist, racist, illiterate and other unflattering afflictions. But this was the only time I was mistaken for an FBI agent.

THE ANECDOTES in this book are similar to the one above, in that most have never been published or received only local attention. When I wrote my sixth book -- "Built to Win" with successful Atlanta Braves general manager and certain future baseball Hall of Fame administrator John Schuerholz – I thought that would be my last project and could enjoy unfettered retirement.

Then I made the mistake of sharing many of these inside stories with friends over dinner. Almost to a person, the reaction was laugh-out-loud, followed by this suggestion: "You need to put all these stories in a book." Haltingly, I penned basic drafts of chapters on Bear Bryant, Mickey Mantle and Shaquille O'Neal and offered one chapter each to three different friends (one a career newspaper editor) to take for a "test read." Their reactions came back in chorus: They all wanted to read more.

One "test reader" was novelist and former *Sentinel* city columnist Bob Morris, who fired off an email slugged: "Icons are freaking hilarious!")

That's when I decided to drag myself out of a very pleasant retirement and complete the manuscript for what I was calling *"Sports Icons R Funny,"* the working title. I hope you will find these stories as amusing and insightful as did my friends.

ACKNOWLEDGEMENTS

HEARTFELT THANKS to many of those icons who not only added details to the anecdotes I recalled, but, after overcoming that knee-jerk brain freeze when asked about their funniest moments, were able to recount additional jocular incidents during their careers. Especially helpful in that vein were Lou Holtz, Steve Sloan, Bobby Bowden, Cris Collinsworth, Davey Johnson and Walt Zembriski. Also helpful were former colleagues who covered or worked for those and other icons. Too numerous to list them all, those helpers included Dolphins exec Harvey Greene, Fort Lauderdale columnist Dave Hyde, longtime Gators beat reporter Chris Harry, Florida State athletics publicist Rob Wilson, Orlando Magic Senior VP Pat Williams, broadcaster Chip Caray, and Atlanta Braves GM John Hart.

Chapter 1 -- Bear Bryant

MY LATE FRIEND Jim Murray, the gifted *Los Angeles Times* sports columnist, once described Paul "Bear" Bryant as "two hundred pounds of wrinkles." Indeed, the legendary football coach at Alabama seemed to be poured into skin two sizes too large for his body. And that only underscored an often hidden amusing aura to the persona of this icon more commonly known as one of the sternest taskmasters in college football history. That side of him could not be described as slapstick, but it was nonetheless *playful*. My very first encounter with Bryant had just that sort of mild mirth to it and set the stage for a privileged relationship I enjoyed with this headline-producing coach right up to his death in 1983.

The occasion was the old Southeastern Conference "Sky-Writers" tour in the early 70s. The tour was an annual 10-day jaunt around the storied Dixie league via an old Southern Airways charter holding about 30 scribes. The tour touched down at each member school during pre-season workouts in August. Each stop included interviews with the coach and prominent players, plus the opportunity to observe a practice session.

(The increasingly paranoid college coaches of today would break out in cold heebie-jeebies at the thought of two dozen or so writers watching their sacrosanct practice sessions.

The caution is greatly overdone; I was one of the few scribes who openly admitted we barely knew what we were looking at in those practices. Barring the sight of the star quarterback showing up on crutches, most writers wouldn't be able to spot anything as meaningful as some exotic play or scheme from watching practice.)

Working for the Jackson (Miss.) *Clarion-Ledger* at the time, I happened to be standing next to Bear's famous coaching tower when the Bama practice was set to commence and the coach began his climb.

Being a young, brash reporter always looking for a different story angle, I asked, "Coach, mind if I join you up there for a few minutes?"

"C'mon," he drawled. "But be careful. This old thing is gettin' a little rickety." I assumed he was talking about the tower.

So up I went and was able to put the readers atop that famous tower, eavesdropping on his commands to the various groups of players sweating below and the jocular dialog between me and The Bear. On the ground, some reporters were indignant. Others were seething. When I came down, one Alabama columnist sharply demanded: "How did you get to go up there??!!"

I shrugged and replied, "Well, I just asked him."

Keep in mind that Bear Bryant was a deity in Alabama and most state sportswriters were so intimidated by his presence, few would have made such a simple request. Charley Thornton, then the sports information director at 'Bama, was not surprised. He explained that many of those state writers would call and ask him to get a comment from the Great Coach if there was some news nugget regarding a player in their circulation area – an injury, promotion to the third-team defense, a solid "C" in freshman English class, whatever.

"I'd always remind the writer that Coach was in his office and available to media calls from noon to 2 and the writer could call for a comment himself," Thornton recounted. "But they'd usually say, 'No, you do it, Charley. I don't want to bother him.' "

That particular approaching season was important because it would open with a rematch against Coach John McKay's vaunted Southern California Trojans. The prior season, the two marquee teams had played in

Birmingham, the first of a 2-year contract. Southern Cal had routed Alabama, 42-21. The victory made a cult hero out of SC running back Sam "Bam" Cunningham, an African-American who humbled 'Bama and The Bear by running for 135 yards and two touchdowns against the all-white Crimson Tide. The coach gave the green light to his coaches to start paying more attention to black prospects after that season.

(McKay and Bryant became good friends, often playing golf and socializing between seasons. McKay recalled being summoned to LAX to meet Bryant's flight after the Bear had enjoyed a couple of days in the Las Vegas casinos. As he was departing, he happened upon newlyweds from Alabama, whom he backed with his own considerable bets at the craps table. The young couple made their point nearly a dozen times in a row, producing a modest stack of chips. Next to them, the Bear was nearly obliterated by a growing pile of chips as he kept letting his winnings double and re-double. When the couple finally passed the dice, Bear cashed in, gave the bride $500 to buy an expensive outfit at the hotel's dress shop, then dashed to the airport to make his flight to L.A.

(When McKay met him at his LAX arrival gate, Bryant, laughing, reached into both pockets of his sport coat and threw up two fistfuls of $100 bills. "I thought sure we were about to be arrested!" McKay recalled.)

When I invaded the revered tower, which had a roof, we shared some kidding banter and I noticed a built-in box that contained just two items. One was a megaphone which he used to bark various instructions, criticisms or commendations to the laboring players and coaches below. The other was a can of wasp spray. "Why wasp spray?" I prodded, like any crack investigative reporter would do.

"Well," he replied in his vibrating *basso profundo* voice, "they sometimes form nests up here under the roof. The little buggers have stung me a few times. But nothing like Southern Cal stung me last year!"

Alabama, with two black starters, would win the rematch, 17-10, in the Los Angeles Coliseum. Bear had installed the Wishbone offense and used it to surprise the Trojans with a 17-0 lead before the USC defense could adjust. The two head coaches had agreed to exchange films of their spring games for scouting purposes, but Bryant craftily waited until August preseason practice to install the Wishbone.

"I forgave him," recalled McKay, "but I didn't forget."

INSTALLING THE WISHBONE offense and integrating his roster shortly after the reign of segregationist Alabama Governor George Wallace were two examples of Bear Bryant's ability to adapt to evolving trends and cultures. Several high-profile Southern coaches were unable to embrace such changes and faded away. Among them was Southern Miss coach Pie Vann, who resisted the inclusion of black players and even made racist remarks to booster clubs while other southern teams were upgrading with talented black athletes. "We are adding a black athlete at Southern," Vann joked to one booster group. "We signed him to a track scholarship - - as a javelin catcher!"

Bryant, meanwhile, made adjustments to accommodate the culture of the growing number of blacks on his team. But he drew the line in the sand at one point over the habit of black players wearing what was called "do-rags" on their heads in practice and games. "I've noticed that some of you boys have taken to wearing these *scar-r-r-rves* on your heads," he disdainfully drawled at a squad meeting, the drawn-out italics his. "I just want to say that's okay with me. You can wear a scarf or a helmet – either one."

The do-rags disappeared for a few Crimson Tide seasons.

AS TIME WENT on, I took Charley Thornton's advice and often called Coach Bryant during that noon-to-two p.m. window to discuss the progress of the football season. I got the feeling he enjoyed bantering with someone who didn't seem to be a total sycophant groveling at his toenails. After I moved to *The Orlando Sentinel*, my new bosses picked up from my scribblings that I had good access to the famous Alabama coach. So they assigned me to cover a game in which Alabama would play host to then-woeful, BBB (before Bobby Bowden) Florida State in Tuscaloosa, primarily to collect material for a lengthy feature story on The Bear.

I called and asked if I could have some time with him in the hours after the mid-afternoon game to flesh out the feature story. With Alabama a 4-touchdown favorite, it figured that he would be in a good mood after the expected rout. But Florida State didn't cooperate. The pesky Seminoles under unconventional new coach Darrell Mudra (he coached from the pressbox, not the sideline) shockingly jumped in front and was still leading late in the second half. Alabama pulled out a narrow victory, but Coach Bryant was mortified at what was nearly a monumental, embarrassing upset.

His somber, irritated comments in the post-game press conference was what you'd expect from a coach who had just lost, 35-0. I figured my appointment to visit him in his home that evening was out the window. At the close of the press conference, I caught his arm and offered that, under the circumstances, we could do the home interview some other time. He shook his head, jotted down his address in my note pad and told me to show up about 7:30.

When I arrived, the Bryants and another couple had finished dinner and were having ice cream while listening to the radio broadcast of an important SEC game matching two of his former players, LSU coach Charlie McClendon and Tennessee coach Bill Battle.

Mary Harmon Bryant, the Bear's firmly protective wife, had greeted me at the door and challenged that maybe I had the wrong Bryant house. "Maybe you want our son, who lives down the street," she suggested. I assured her I had the right Bryant, and showed her the address he had written for me. She closed the door and I stood there blinking a few moments until she came back, opened the door and graciously welcomed me.

After the ice cream, the LSU-Tennessee game reached halftime and Coach Bryant ushered me into his study for our rambling interview. I kept noticing over his shoulder a framed, abstract painting that seemed vaguely familiar. I asked him about it. "Some guy painted it and sent it to me. Mary Harmon framed it and hung it up in here," he said with a shrug, as if it were of little consequence.

I asked to take a closer look and it suddenly hit me: It was one of the many paintings *Sports Illustrated* had commissioned, to use as cover art for their issues on major sports events – The Super Bowl, World Series, NBA Finals, Masters, Kentucky Derby, etc. This particular one depicted Alabama's deciding touchdown in an epic game against Tennessee. The "some guy" was legendary sports artist LeRoy Neiman.

There over Bear's shoulder was a near-priceless oil by LeRoy Neiman.

Some guy.

BEAR BRYANT wore a conspicuous bandage on his nose that day and still had it on at home that evening. Somebody had asked him about it during the post-game press conference and he managed to chuckle and claim: "It's nothing. It's where Mary Harmon hit me with a fryin' pan."

But during our conversation in his study, he said, "Don't use this in your story . . . ," and proceeded to reveal the bandage was to conceal where he had a skin cancer removed the previous day. I could tell he was somewhat emotional as he emphasized the tissues removed were confirmed to be malignant. He explained there had been a lot of cancer in his family tree and he was definitely concerned.

Skin cancers, as I was made to understand, can spread to more serious locations, but are generally controlled by the simple removal. My mind sped up to 100 rpm. Here was the thunderclap news that the most prominent name in college football apparently thinks he had only months to live and the information was off the record. I stayed over in Tuscaloosa long enough on Sunday to write the feature for Monday's editions of the *Sentinel*, mentioning only Coach Bryant's flippant frying pan remark and nothing about Big C.

I flew home that evening and met Monday morning with my managing editor, a terrific newsman named Stan Roberts, to tell him all about the skin cancer and the coach's off-the-record doomsday reaction. Roberts said it was too big a story to sit on, informed me that we should print the story and, if I felt it would compromise my ethics, I could correctly relate that my boss "took" the story from me and ordered me to write it.

The story was picked up by the wire services and created national waves. Coach Bryant was inundated by phone calls and messages from friends and relatives and media all across the country. I faxed a heart-felt letter to him, saying I felt awful about the distractions it was causing and apologized for not refusing the order to write the story. I didn't hear back, at least not immediately. The furor eased when medics assured him all cancer cells had been removed and promised he would live to win many more bowls and championships.

A few months later, the Southeastern Conference winter meetings were held in Orlando at Arnold Palmer's Bay Hill Club and Lodge. The annual event includes SEC presidents, athletic directors and head football and basketball coaches. One of the ironic usual topics was how to cut back expenses for their athletic programs, while gathered at some of the most expensive golf resorts in the South. Bay Hill. The Breakers. Sandestin. Sea Island. (I suspect if some athletic director had proposed holding the meeting at a Holiday Inn somewhere to cut costs, he or she would have been drummed out of the Conference.)

I happened to be in the Bay Hill lobby when a limo pulled up and out unfolded Paul Bear Bryant Himself. When he saw me, he headed straight to where I stood, while I mentally reviewed my blood type and life insurance coverage. He stuck out a huge paw, shook my hand and said, simply, "Larry, how are you? We gonna play a little golf here this week?" Somebody handed him his room key and he sauntered off as a bit of color came back to my face.

Clearly, what had happened was that he showed me all was forgiven and we were still friends – despite the disruption in his life caused, in part, by me printing a story he asked me not to. At that moment, Coach Bryant became one of the athletic figures I would admire for having the unique ability not to hold a grudge when unpleasantness temporarily challenged a relationship.

Miami Dolphins Coach Don Shula, NCAA basketball champion coach Norm Sloan, Yankees icon George Steinbrenner, Florida State coach Bobby Bowden are prominent on my short list.

BEAR BRYANT liked Bay Hill and the nearby dog track (Bear and his family owned one not far from Tuscaloosa) and returned at least once every off-season. He'd typically call me to set up a golf game and allowed me and my wife to pick him up for dinner at one of our favorite Orlando eateries.

One place was La Cantina, a frumpy little steak house (later replaced with a larger, opulent facility) where Central Florida power brokers liked to frequent and kibitz with colorful owner Al Seng. Al was the chief cook and his wife, Linda, ran the dining room. When they were still in the cramped, first location, Orlando status was defined by whether you were on "Al's list," which allowed you to enter through the kitchen back door, have a drink and carry on with Al while waiting for the first available table. The "regular" folk waiting on the sidewalk outside the front entrance would just have to bide their time.

Seng, an avid college football fan, was clearly thrilled when I popped through the back door one evening with Bear Bryant in tow. Al poured himself and the coach a drink from the bottle of black Jack Daniels he kept on a shelf over the grill and the two of them launched a jocular debate about the best ways to cook a steak.

(Al became so enamored by Bear that he forked over a lot of money to purchase a commemorative bronze bust of Bear in his signature houndstooth hat. The bust occupied a place of honor over the bar in the new building, where it remained until Al and Linda divorced. She kept the restaurant, Al took the Bear.)

The evening had started with me picking up the coach at a Bay Hill cottage only to walk in on another medical situation. Coach Bryant typically traveled with a pleasant black man, Billy Varner, whom the University had hired as Bear's personal driver and security assistant. Billy's main assignment each time they came to Orlando was to pick up a program for the Sanford-Orlando Kennel Club's evening races. Together, they would handicap the entries and Bear would circle his choices for Billy to bet. He'd give Billy a large fold of money to place the wagers at the track while Bear was out to dinner.

On this particular evening, however, Billy was faced with another daunting task. It seems an intruder bee had gotten into the cottage and stung the coach near his navel as he exited the shower. It befell Billy's duty to extract the stinger. That was the scene as I entered the room – the famed coach lying on his back, his belly rising and falling with laughter as poor Billy struggled to remove the dancing stinger. The only thing missing was Leroy Neiman to capture the sniggering moment.

OF ALL THE favored 'Bear's boys,' Steve Sloan, road-game roommate of the famed Joe Namath, was near the top of the list. Sloan played and coached under Bryant and was tapped by the Coach to be his successor when time came to retire. (More about that later.) A defensive back and quarterback, Sloan was a veritable pipe cleaner by body type, but a gifted athlete and tough. "Tough as a skinned mule," Coach Bryant liked to say. (Old Nosy Here once asked him what a skinned mule was and what made it so tough. He laughed and said, "That's just a sayin' we used to have back in Moro Bottom (Arkansas)."

The humble, engaging Sloan, now retired in Orlando, was and remains deeply respectful of Coach Bryant and vows he was the greatest motivator of athletes and staff he'd ever been around. Even when it cost Sloan his six front teeth.

Bama was undefeated midway through the '64 season when they made the short trip to Starkville, Mississippi, to play what was then one of the league's lesser teams, Mississippi State, with Sloan at the controls and Namath nursing a knee injury. State didn't win many games during that era, but they were known for their tough, hard-hitting defense. "And they didn't like quarterbacks," Sloan muses.

With a small lead in the third quarter, Sloan ran a quarterback keeper to the sideline where he was blasted by a State linebacker and knocked *under* the Alabama bench. His helmet flew off and a telephone cord – communication to coaches in the pressbox – was wrapped around his neck. As he struggled to get untangled and back on his feet, he discovered his mouth was bloodied and team trainer Jim Goosetree rushed to investigate. The Bear quickly interceded, shoving Goosetree aside, and asked Sloan what was the problem.

"I think I hurt my mouth," he said, wiping away blood.

"Lemme see," said the Coach, who peeled back Sloan's upper lip and rendered his diagnosis: "It's just a chipped tooth." With that settled, he sent Sloan back onto the field. ("I don't think we even took a timeout. It all happened that fast," Sloan recently recalled.)

Alabama held on for a 23-6 victory and retreated to the visiting team's locker room, typically stark and uninviting dungeons in those days. Sloan, his mouth throbbing, found a broken, triangular piece of mirror taped to a wall and took a look at the damage. He was shocked to discover his six front teeth were either broken or knocked out completely. Haltingly, he went to the coaches' dressing room to seek The Coach.

"I never tried to initiate a conversation with Coach," Sloan noted. "But this time, well, I said, 'Coach, I just looked in the mirror and I've lost, basically, all of my front teeth.' He said, 'Well, I'll tell you what I'll do. I'll buy you some new teeth on Monday.' I said, 'Fine.' End of conversation."

Sloan still sports that gleaming white row of six Bear teeth at the top of his ever-ready smile.

DRAFTED BY the NFL Atlanta Falcons, Sloan played sparingly before tearing his rotator cuff in his second season. Bryant reached out and pulled one of his favorite pupils back to Tuscaloosa – as the Crimson Tides' newest quarterbacks coach. "Twelve thousand dollars a year," Sloan remembers. "He offered me nine, but I got him up to a thousand dollars a month."

With that, Sloan fared better in negotiations with Coach Bryant than some other prominent staffers. Charlie McClendon, who would later enjoy great success as head coach at LSU, felt he was being grossly underpaid as a young assistant coach under Bear Bryant at Kentucky. "Charlie Mac" marched into Bryant's office and said he was not being paid enough to live on. "If I wanted to pay you more," McClendon recalled Coach Bryant snorting, "I would have. Now get out of here and get back to work." Both are gone now, but the two men maintained an endearing personal relationship over the ensuing years.

Bear's staff meetings were a wonder to Sloan, mesmerized by Coach's Bryant's deft cajoling of his assistants to give their very best. The assistant coaches went to great lengths to impress the boss, even to reporting for duty long before sunup.

At one point, two assistants, Ken Donahue and Bob Tyler, tried to be the first to turn on the lights. Donahue was the avowed champ of pre-dawn starts. Determined, Tyler kept showing up 15 minutes earlier each day to no avail. When he reported for duty at 4:15 one morning and found Donahue already hard at work breaking down game films, Tyler threw in the towel and went back to a seven a.m. start.

In his third year on staff, Sloan was given the game-day assignment of calling plays from the pressbox. He'd phone down to the sideline the next play or make a player substitution through another assistant, Jimmy Sharpe, who would then send in the play or substitute.

"When Joe and I were the quarterbacks, we called our own plays. So this was something of a new trend, especially to Coach Bryant," says Sloan. "It was kinda funny in one respect. If the play I called worked, Coach would just stare ahead. But if the play didn't work, he'd turn around and look up at the pressbox with a scowl. I'd sort of try to duck down behind the counter."

At the end of that 1970 season, in the Bluebonnet Bowl in Houston against the Oklahoma Sooners, things got a little bizarre. Sloan's communication from the pressbox was almost exclusively to Sharpe. But during the close game, Bryant, who was going for his 200th career win, took the headset from Sharpe and instructed Sloan: "We gotta get (Ron) Durby in the game!"

You never told Coach Bryant you couldn't do as he instructed, but in this case Sloan was conflicted as to what to say. But Durby, a very good offensive tackle in his day, had graduated five years earlier and Sloan knew at that time Durby was a lawyer (and later a judge) in Chattanooga. "I said, 'Coach, I don't know if we can do that or not.' Well, that was the wrong thing to say. About five or six strong words from him and I was made to understand that we had to get Ron Durby in the game. I looked all around in the pressbox to see if Durby was there. What is funny is that Coach never mentioned that again. Nor did I."

During the 1964 season, when Sloan was filling in for the injured Namath in a game against Florida, Coach Bryant made a post-game comment that Sloan says illustrates that the Coach had a "way" or aura, about him. Trailing Alabama, 17-14, in the closing seconds, Florida chose to try a short field goal and tie the game, rather than going for a touchdown and the victory. Sloan recalls standing on the sideline, *knowing* the kick would be good. Since overtime hadn't been introduced to college football at that time, it would have ended in a tie. But Florida missed the short field goal and Alabama won. In the locker room after the game, Sloan happened to be near Coach when a reporter asked: "Coach Bryant, what would have happened had they made that field goal?"

"And this is poignant," Sloan continues the tale. "Coach had this look about him when someone asked a stupid question. He gave the guy that look and said, 'If the field goal had been good, we would'a blocked it!' That's the way he thought."

SLOAN RECALLED another anecdote with a religious aspect. A strong Christian and daily reader of the Bible, he had taken the job of offensive coordinator at Georgia Tech and was heavily involved in recruiting after that first season, working 14 hours a day. A call came in from Coach Bryant, who was attending the national college football coaches' convention in Chicago. He wanted to know if he could ask Sloan a question. "Of course," Sloan assured. "Go right ahead, Coach."

"No, I want to ask you in person. Get on a plane and come up here to Chicago."

Sloan protested that he was dog tired and in the middle of recruiting and hadn't planned to attend the meeting in Chicago.

"No, you come up here tomorrow. I've got an important question to ask you," the Coach persisted.

Sloan sighed and agreed. Next day, he flew to Chicago, took a cab to Coach Bryant's hotel and went to his room. "In the Christian faith," the coach began, "how does a man's works come into it?" (Many believe a person's good works while alive are enough to make it to heaven, whether or not they had formally accepted Jesus Christ as their savior.)

There was a Gideon Bible in the room and Sloan opened it to Ephesians 2: 8-9 and read: *For it is by grace you have been saved through faith, and this not from yourselves. It is the gift of God. Not by works so that no one can boast.*

"So no matter what you do, salvation's grace is a gift," Sloan explained.

The Coach pondered that a moment and said, "Okay. Thanks."

With that, Sloan cabbed to the airport and flew back to Atlanta. All on his own dime, of course. And that was fine. Whatever Coach wanted, Sloan was all too willing to provide.

EXCEPT ON one occasion. Bryant heard that Sloan had been offered the head coach job at Vanderbilt, the SEC's long-running football doormat. He called and said he assumed Sloan would resign as a Georgia Tech assistant and take the head job at Vanderbilt. Sloan noted that legendary former Tech coach, Bobby Dodd, had advised him not to take the job at what many considered was a coaching graveyard.

"No, you're gonna take the job," Bryant insisted.

"Well, Coach ---"

"What'd you say?" Bryant interrupted firmly.

"I think that's a good idea," relented Sloan and was head coach at Vandy the next three seasons, leading the Commodores to their first two bowl appearances in decades. Impressed, Texas Tech lured him away and a couple of years into that stint, Coach Bryant called to make him a secret promise that has long remained the subject of rumor and speculation.

"He told me he would be retiring the next year and that I would get the (Alabama) job," Sloan recently affirmed in an interview for this book. A year passed and he heard nothing further, so when Sloan was offered the job of head coach at Ole Miss he accepted. Bryant called as soon as he heard the news. Three decades later, Sloan recalls the dialog as if yesterday.

"Listen, I heard you're going to Ole Miss."

"Yes, sir."

"No. I want you to take this job instead."

"Coach, I've already told them I accepted. I can't just back out."

"Awwww, they won't care."

Sloan kept his word to Ole Miss and spent the next five years trying to rebuild that once-proud football program when he could have inherited the gilded throne at his alma mater. "Well, I wouldn't have been a good replacement for him," Sloan now rationalizes the only time when he chose not to follow the Bear's personal dictum.

BEAR BRYANT had that kind of sway over many individuals, bowl committees, the Southeastern Conference and even the mothership NCAA. For several years, Bryant had a policy designed to keep his players in touch with their families back home. As players reported for practice, they would be greeted at least once a week by a stack of penny post cards at the equipment room door. They were permitted to pick up their laundered practice uniforms only after they had jotted a note to their parents and turned in the cards for mailing.

An overzealous NCAA investigator got wind of the practice and sent Bryant a terse letter of warning that the post cards violated the NCAA's "extra benefits" rule. The coach arranged for a telephone to be installed in the squad meeting room, noting to an administrator that he wanted to make an important phone call in front of his players.

The squad buzzed curiously as Bryant dialed the NCAA investigator. "This is Coach Bryant at Alabama," he began. "I got your letter about these post cards. I just wanted to let you know that if you consider that a violation, you may as well go ahead and punish us. Because I'm not gonna stop having these boys write home to their mamas." He hung up and the players smiled, ear to ear.

Some years later, when I heard the story, I asked him about it. Bear Bryant responded with a sly smile and a twinkle in his eyes: "I never heard another word from that gentleman."

Chapter 2 – Mickey Mantle

IT WAS WHILE Mickey Mantle was limping through his final couple of seasons that I had the opportunity to participate in a few locker room interviews of Mantle along with a gaggle of other journalists. The first time I truly met Mickey and interacted with him on a personal level was a few years later when we played golf at the exclusive Preston Trail Golf Club a short distance north of downtown Dallas.

Preston Trail is an all-men's club where the membership was dominated by wealthy oil men during the last half of the 20th century. Tour star Lanny Wadkins was a notable member, along with the iconic centerfielder, famed No. 7, of the New York Yankees. That was before BMW, Mercedes-Benz and Lexus elbowed their way into the American luxury car market. Back then, the overprivileged traversed the streets of Dallas almost exclusively in Cadillacs. That fact spawned the following, fabled exchange between a couple of Preston Trail members that may or may not have actually happened:

"Well, I bought a new car today."

"Yeah? What kind did you get?"

"Blue."

I played Preston Trail that fateful day in 1976 as guest of Ron Meyer shortly after he took over as head football coach at nearby Southern Methodist University. The club roster was liberally dotted with well-heeled SMU Mustang grads and boosters, who would help Meyer land SMU football in the NCAA jailhouse. Those Mustang elders not only chipped in to buy a club membership for Meyer, but, according to NCAA sleuths, also a few quarterbacks, linebackers and an all-Galaxy halfback or two.

On the putting green, Meyer was given an impromptu welcome to the club by Mantle and a friend of his, whose name escapes me. Mickey suggested we play as a foursome and off we went. At the time, Preston Trail's front nine was bordered by a number of posh homes, while the back nine was totally secluded, winding through thick hammocks of huge oak trees. This was when Mickey was into his one-beer-per-hole period, before he belatedly sobered up in an attempt to de-pickle his kidneys. So it was beer and giggles most of the way around.

Then it got interesting. On one tee on the secluded nine, Mickey laughed and asked if we were willing to play "Double Oklahoma" on that hole. I was familiar with the old golf ruse that if you play "Oklahoma rules" and fail to advance your drive past the women's tee (which were non- existent at Preston), you had to play the remainder of that hole with your fly unzipped. But "Double Oklahoma" was new to me. I turned to Coach Meyer to see what he knew. He shrugged, palms up, indicating this was new to him, too. But being a good sport, Meyer nodded and said, "That's fine, Mickey. Double Oklahoma it is!"

Mantle often teed off with a 2-iron because he said his driver "behaves worse than Billy Martin." But on this hole, Mickey decided to go with the driver and blasted a moon shot deep into the oaks. He needed two chips to get back on the fairway, followed by a chunked approach that failed to clear White Rock Creek that meanders through the course. We eventually conceded him a 4-foot putt that gave him a total of eight on the hole, which was the high score in our foursome. Thus, Mickey Mantle suffered the wrath of Double Oklahoma.

He had to play the next hole wearing only his golf spikes and a silly grin.

That left Preston neophyte Meyer in wide-eyed shock at first, then transitioned to laughter until Mantle put his clothes back on at the next tee. Other Preston members would not have been surprised, given their knowledge of Mickey's legendary immodesty in clubhouses – whether golf or baseball.

A friend of mine, Will Jarrett, who owned a chain of small newspapers, joined Preston Trail some years later and said he was told there were basically only two rules at Preston. One, you are not allowed to drive your golf cart within the leather. Two (known as the Mickey Mantle Rule), you must wear SOMETHING in the men's grill. It seems Mickey was in the habit of emerging from the shower room, stepping into a pair of flip-flops and walking into the grill *au naturel* to slap together a sandwich off the buffet – wearing only that aforementioned grin and the shower shoes.

Fortunately, Mickey had already retired before the Yankees were forced by court order to admit female sport writers into their post-game locker room. It would be another Mickey who bared his privates when that happened. But more about that later in this chapter.

Aside from becoming familiar with the Double Oklahoma rule, I also learned that day that Mickey had a couple of scheduled endorsement appearances on his upcoming schedule in Orlando where I was based. He asked if I knew anyone who could get him on Arnold Palmer's famed Bay Hill Club, which he had long wanted to play. Easy. I was a member of Bay Hill at the time and would be more than happy to host him for a game during his visit. So it was set that I would pick him up at the airport, take him to a hotel conference center where, in a natty, three-piece suit, he would put on an indoor batting clinic for dozens of gawking young boys and extoll the wonders of his sponsor-of-the-day, a European vacuum cleaner.

The round of golf at Bay Hill was G-rated, what with my advisory that Double Oklahoma might not be acceptable at Arnie's place. What was more interesting was the greeting at the airport. This was back in the good old simple days when you could go all the way to the concourse gate to greet an arriving friend or relative. When the jetway door opened, out came Mickey and a gaggle of businessmen, all laughing and patting Mickey on the back.

"Looks like you guys have been partying all the way from Dallas," I conjectured. But the frivolity had begun only moments before as the plane taxied in from the main runway.

For such quick trips, Mickey usually traveled with just a briefcase holding nothing but eight-by-ten glossies of himself in Yankee uniform and a couple of felt-tipped markers for autographing. After all, that was exactly what people wanted when bumping into The Mick. While he signed several of the photos for men in his first-class cabin, the attractive young stewardess became curious.

"You must be someone famous," she said.

"Nah. Just an old broken-down ex-ballplayer," chuckled Mickey, ever the flirt. "But, here, I'll sign one for you."

Mickey jotted her name, autographed the photo, added a phone number and handed it to her. "Now it's your turn. Here, sign my cocktail napkin," he said.

"But I'm not famous," she countered.

"Doesn't matter. What's fair is fair. I signed for you. Now you should sign for me."

Somewhat reluctantly, she scrawled her name on the napkin and handed it to Mickey. "But go ahead and put your phone number on it like I did."

The other men gave their full attention to the exchange as her eyes narrowed suspiciously as she asked, "Why? Do you have a son my age?"

Mickey and the businessmen were still laughing as they exited the plane. When he repeated the episode to me in the gate area, he underscored the stew's put-down by wrapping his hands around the shaft of an imaginary spear and shoved it into his chest. "WHUMP!!" he laughed while the businessmen giggled anew and nodded their affirmation.

IT WAS NO SECRET that Mickey was a womanizer both as a player and later as a handsome forty-something in retirement. Owner George Steinbrenner provided me with a copy of a document that quietly circulated among a few baseball insiders.

The year was 1972 and the Yankees management began preparing for a very special, season-long celebration the next year. Yankees public relations director Bob Fishel, who would later become an official in the Commissioner's Office, sent out the following letter to prominent current and past Yankee players:

Dear Mickey,

As you probably know, 1973 marks the 50th anniversary of Yankee Stadium and we are going to have a season-long Golden Anniversary celebration. We hope to mark the occasion on our Old Timers Day, Saturday, August 11, as well as on individual dates during the season.

We thought it would be interesting to learn from you what you consider your outstanding event at Yankee Stadium. In many cases the answer is obvious, but because we are writing a large number of your former teammates, we are asking to answer this question for us.

Nineteen seventy-three will be the final season at Yankee Stadium as we know it. We will be located at Shea in 1974 and '75 while Yankee Stadium is completely rebuilt to reopen in 1976. Thanks for your cooperation. We are looking forward to seeing you in 1973 and wish you a happy holiday season.

Very truly yours,

(signed) Bob Fishel

December 14, 1972

Mickey filled in and returned the questionnaire as follows:

I consider the following my outstanding experience at Yankee Stadium:

(response) *"I had (sex) under the right field bleachers by the Yankee bullpen."*

This event occurred on or about (Give as much detail as you can):

(response) *"It was about the third or fourth inning. I had a pulled groin and couldn't play at the time and spent the game in our bullpen. She was a very nice girl. . ."* Mickey went on to provide lurid details and some dialog he had with the girl during his "outstanding experience." He signed the form as follows:

"Mickey Mantle, the All-American Boy"

THAT OTHER immodest Mickey mentioned previously in this chapter was precocious Mickey Rivers, a speedy, slap hitter who played centerfield for the Yankees several seasons long after Mantle had retired in 1969. In 1978, militant feminist Melissa Ludtke Lincoln, then a reporter for *Sports Illustrated*, sued the Yankees and major league baseball for the right of female sportswriters to enter the post-game locker rooms for interviews along with their male counterparts.

District Court Judge Constance Baker granted Melissa a court-ordered injunction forcing baseball to provide equal locker room access to sportswriters regardless of gender, just in time for Game 3 of the 1978 World Series between the Yankees and the Los Angeles Dodgers at Yankees Stadium. Yankees owner George Steinbrenner dealt with the sticky situation by providing small wrap-around, terry cloth garments that the players could snap around their waists upon exiting the shower room.

I was among the mass of scribes who – along with Melissa Ludtke Lincoln - - flocked into the Yankees' locker room to witness the historic and amusing scene of scattered Yankees players being interviewed while wearing what looked like terry cloth miniskirts. However, one player declined to wear the special garment. Rivers, defiantly wearing nothing at all, shadowed Melissa from locker to locker, swinging his manhood side to side. "Hey, girlie!" he taunted the distaff invader. "You know what this is?"

Melissa countered with: "It looks like a penis, only smaller." Laughter erupted and Rivers' face turned roughly the color of beets.

Chapter 3 – Shaquille O'Neal

A SINGLE anecdote underscores why basketball giant Shaquille O'Neal was considered the quintessential "man-child." It was a few days before his Orlando Magic took on the Chicago Bulls in the NBA playoffs. Shaq lived in a mansion in the toney Isleworth Country Club community. In front was his security gate which he had modestly festooned with the "Superman" emblem. Out back was the expansive Lake Butler Chain, one of his favorite playgrounds.

Shaq loved to skip along the lake on his wave runner, darting here and there like some oversized water bug behind the large homes on the shoreline. A young neighbor, 12-year-old Jason English, regularly navigated the lake in a small boat with an outboard motor. Shaq and Jason had met out on the lake one afternoon and developed a little game that Shaq loved: Jason would go round and round in a tight circle, churning the surface of the lake in preparation for Shaq to charge through the middle of the circle, bouncing along the created waves.

Peggy English, Jason's mom, responded to her front door bell one day, swinging open the ornate entry. Standing there, taking up nearly all of the opening and blotting out the Florida sun, was the 7-foot-1, 325-pounds of toned muscle, Shaquille O'Neal, wearing his swim trunks and a wide grin. "You think Jason wants to come out to play?" he asked, hope spreading across his countenance.

The first pick in the 1992 NBA draft out of LSU by the Orlando Magic, Shaq quickly became one of the league's superstars and a global favorite of young fans. Most any 12-year-old in America would have excitedly given up their PlayStation had Shaq shown up at their door in need of a playmate.

Amused, Peggy English said she would have to check. While Shaq stood there at the door, she walked to the den and announced that Shaq had arrived, wanting to play. Jason, who was watching cartoons on television, wrinkled his nose in contemplation for a moment before declining the opportunity.

Peggy returned to the front door and advised her huge and famous neighbor that Jason was busy watching TV and wasn't in the mood to play. Shaq's wide shoulders slumped in disappointment as he turned and retreated to his own manse.

THE MAGIC management also discovered in their very first face-to-face encounter with Shaq that he was not exactly a mature adult. When the team pulled the right ping-pong ball to win the lottery for the 1992 NBA draft, it was widely assumed that the team had won the big prize for that draft – the overpowering LSU center, Shaquille O'Neal. But there were some strange and iffy moments before the draft.

First, the Magic managed to put on a dog-and-pony show for Shaq's Los Angeles-based agent, Leonard Armato, underscoring the wonders of Central Florida and the strength of the team ownership. But team officials were having trouble arranging a visit by Shaq and his family to Orlando. Word filtered back that Armato was keeping them at arm's length while exploring any possible deal that might land his celebrated client on the West Coast. Had he pulled it off, Armato would have become an instant celebrity in L.A., and doubtless could have commanded the best table at any restaurant he chose.

Finally, Shaq & Co., agreed to come to Orlando to discuss the likely prospect that the team would choose him with that golden first pick in the approaching NBA draft, which at that point was only days away. A dinner was arranged next door to Orlando Arena in the dining room at the Marriott Hotel, where the entourage would be camped. Everyone would have a chance to get to know one another and all would be peachy.

The dinner party numbered about a dozen, including Magic Coach Matty Guokas, Magic GM Pat Williams, Magic exec John Gabriel (who would later rise to GM), team owner and billionaire Amway co-founder Rich DeVos and his wife Helen, Armato, Shaq's parents, Lucille and Phillip Harrison, and his younger brother Jamaal, who was about 13 at the time. Shaq and Jamaal were at one end of the table along with Guokas and Williams. The others were ensconced elsewhere along the lengthy table.

The table was in an alcove of the main dining room, but not totally hidden from public view. "It was not formal or private," recalls Gabriel, "but an impressive and dignified gathering, including Mr. DeVos, one of the country's most prestigious businessmen/entrepreneurs."

Some in the Magic entourage noticed that Shaq and Jamaal began to playfully reach over and grab food items off of one another's plate. That escalated to dinner rolls thrown at one another. That escalated to a full-blown food fight, Shaq and Jamaal firing baked potatoes and other parts of their entrees at each another.

Seated in the closest ringside seats for this shocking affront to Emily Post, Williams and Guokas blinked and exchanged expressions of disbelief. Lucille spoke sternly to the combatants and at least a temporary truce was declared in the flying groceries war.

When the dinner ended and the Magic contingent was walking away from the hotel, Guokas reflected on the bizarre behavior. "When the food started flying, I didn't know what to think or how to handle that," he said, adding through a grin: "I was very tempted to send both of them upstairs to their rooms."

Says Gabriel: "It gave us some insight into the level of immaturity we would be dealing with."

THERE WERE TIMES that immaturity played out in a shameful manner, and at other times in plain good-natured humor. It was shameful when he stiffed a terminal young boy who was granted his dream of meeting Shaq through arrangements by the Magic and the Make-a-Wish Foundation. When time came after practice for Shaq to go into a nearby room to greet the boy and his parents, Shaq instead peeled off a $100 bill and thrust it at a Magic official. "Here, give this to the kid. I don't feel like doing this today," Shaq said as he exited the arena gym without meeting the dying lad.

It was also shameful when an English female reporter from the British Broadcasting Company questioned Shaq at his locker during post-game interviews one evening. Shaq sat on the stool in front of his locker wearing only a towel draped across his lap. As he gave mundane answers to the naïve woman's queries, Shaq kept inching the towel higher on his thighs in an obvious attempt to "accidentally" flash her with his manhood. When he caught the eye of a male reporter who realized what was happening, Shaq quickly returned the towel to its original position and abandoned the ploy.

But it was charitable and appreciated when he sang at some strangers' wedding at an Allentown, Pa. hotel in which the Magic team, the rock group Marilyn Manson, performers in the Sesame Street Ice Follies and the wedding party were all snowed in. The Magic had flown from Cleveland to Pennsylvania to play the Philadelphia 76ers, but the team's charter jet was diverted to Allentown by an historic blizzard. "There was two to three feet of snow. The game was canceled and no one could get to our hotel or leave," recalled then-Magic Coach Brian Hill. The niece of famed football legend Johnny Unitas was the bride and her maids of honor were all there, but only a few of the wedding guests could get to the hotel. So the Magic team was invited and, with little else to do, attended.

Shaq made the ceremony memorable with an impromptu song he dedicated to the bride and groom, while several of his teammates lusted after the maids of honor (except for forward Horace Grant, who reserved his unwholesome suggestive comments for the attractive bride).

The team was stranded at the Allentown Hilton for three days before the storm abated enough for them to fly out. Asked about the highlight of the unscheduled stay in Allentown, Magic TV play-by-play announcer Chip Caray replied: "Leaving."

It was also playful and funny when the team arrived in Sacramento, CA., to play the Kings. The usual knot of autograph hounds was camped at the front door of the hotel when the team bus pulled up. One by one, Magic players disembarked, but the autograph-seekers held out for the big prize – Shaquille O'Neal's signature. Shaq sat at the very back of the bus and was last to get off, wearing dark glasses and an oversized blond wig with long yellow curls hanging down. With a giggle, Hill recalled: "Despite being seven-foot and 300 pounds, he walked right past all of the autograph hounds, who just stood there and kept waiting for Shaq to get off the bus."

But it wasn't playful and funny when Shaq evoked a fight with team leader and point guard Scott Skiles during a West Coast road trip. The team was thumped so badly by the Los Angeles Lakers, Coach Brian Hill ordered the team back into The Forum late the next morning for a full-scale practice before flying on to Sacramento. A scrimmage was held with emphasis on defense, but some players were merely going through the motions when the feisty Skiles admonished his teammates with: "Are we going to work on this or are we just going to act like a bunch of pussies!?"

Shaq fired back, using the nickname the team gave Skiles for his resemblance to the infamous horror-film doll: "F--- you, Chuckie! You're the one who caused all of this!" Skiles, who never backed down from anyone, physically challenged Shaq, giving up about 125 pounds and a foot in height. They went at it, Shaq mostly backing away and fending off Skiles' punches. Teammates shuffled around the pair as the scrum moved across the playing floor, knocking over several courtside chairs. "I was mostly punching UP," said Skiles, who would spend the recent 2015-16 season as Magic coach. "But I got in a couple of shots."

The Miami Heat, which was to play the Lakers the next night, had entered the building for a scheduled practice session and laughed from the stands as the Magic melee careened around the court like a rugby scrum.

AS A ROOKIE, Shaq predictably turned out to be prime fodder for veteran Detroit Pistons center Bill Laimbeer, whose goal in life apparently was to frustrate young opponents with disrespectful smack talk and Academy Award-winning "flops" to draw unwarranted personal fouls against them. In their earlier meetings during the 92-93 season, Laimbeer had plied his tactics with moderate success against Shaq. But in an April, late-season game when the Magic were on the cusp of making the playoffs, Laimbeer turned up the heat and climbed into Shaq's head big time at Orlando's "O-rena."

Boston Celtic executive Jan Volk was probably right in referring to Laimbeer as "the ultimate provocateur." Also correct was that Shaq's immature persona made him the league's most vulnerable target for Laimbeer's taunting and gamesmanship. At the slightest bump from Shaq, Laimbeer would dramatically sail backwards, landing on the parquet floor in his well-rehearsed, signature "flop." He was convincing enough in the eyes of the referees that Shaq was quickly in foul trouble and had to sit on the bench for several long stretches to keep from prematurely fouling out of this key game. The first time Shaq was fouled, sending him to the free-throw line, Laimbeer made the most of Shaq's reputation as a scatter-shot free-throw shooter.

(He was so bad at the free-throw line that when he was several minutes late for tipoff of one home game, some unkind columnist wrote the next morning the reason Shaq was tardy was that he took a local toll road to the arena and his quarters kept bouncing off the toll bucket.)

As Shaq toed the line and players from both teams positioned themselves along the foul lane, Laimbeer teased loud enough for all to hear: "Boy, *this* ought to be fun to watch!" Shaq visibly tensed at the taunting comment, his eyes narrowing in angry concentration. He heaved a line-drive free throw attempt that missed miserably. Laimbeer laughed pointedly, inspiring Shaq to throw up another brick. The Pistons grabbed the rebound and Laimbeer jogged off to the other end giggling alongside a red-faced Shaq.

As the game progressed, Shaq became more and more discombobulated as Laimbeer relentlessly plied his craft on the big man's brain. Shaq so lost his composure that during a scramble for a loose rebound, he balled up his fist and struck Piston Alvin Robertson in the back of his head. The refs tossed Shaq for the punch and the next day the league fined him $10,000 and suspended him from the next game. He had left the Detroit game with just 7 points – his season low – and now would be missing in action for the next game that was vital to his team's playoff chances.

NATURALLY, all of us smart-alecks on press row, who had a front-row seat to observe the lobotomy Laimbeer had performed on Shaq, were not properly sympathetic to the big man. I penned a column that appeared the next morning after the Detroit game, taking editorial sport regarding the way Laimbeer had crawled inside Shaq's head and disrupted all the gears and pinwheels until Shaq self-destructed.

As I entered the locker room after practice that next day, Shaq pointed a long, long finger at me over the heads of several writers gathered at his locker. If you listen closely, you might get the idea that he didn't appreciate my sniggering prose. "YOU!" he thundered. "I read that shit you wrote this morning and I'm not speaking to you for a month!"

Amused, I strolled over to his locker and countered, "Gee, Shaq. Was any of that shit wrong?" The gathered writers allowed themselves subdued snickers. Shaq only scowled.

"And tell me," I continued. "You slip out the back door to avoid all of us media after many games. You've returned none of the half-dozen or so calls I've made to your house. You stood me up for an appointed interview in the team hotel when I went with the team all the way to San Antonio just to do a story celebrating your birthday.

"So, tell me, Shaq. If you're not going to talk to me for a month, how will I be able to tell?"

Dennis Scott, Shaq's best friend on the team, fell back into his locker, holding a towel over his face to keep the big man from seeing him laughing. Even Shaq couldn't resist a small smile at the irony.

But, somehow, I would have to write daily columns for the next month without the benefit of Shaquille O'Neal's insightful wisdom.

And with Shaq forced to watch the next game from the bench in his civvies, the Magic barely missed a playoff berth.

SHAQ'S MOST NOTABLE unexcused absence came several days after his grandmother passed away in New Jersey. Shaq was permitted to attend the funeral, of course, but not the days and days afterward when no one connected with the team was able to make contact with him. As it turned out, Shaq had chosen an unusual venue and method to exercise his extended "grieving period."

After Shaq had missed two Magic games, I received a call from an old friend, former Atlanta sports writer Ron Hudspeth, who was producing a regular tabloid covering Atlanta's lively nightlife. Ron wanted to know why Shaq, for the two previous nights, was hanging out in an Atlanta nightclub infamous for its shapely and accommodating NBA groupies. I passed along the sighting to the Magic, who passed it along to Shaq's mother, Lucille, who dialed her AWOL son's cell phone.

She sternly admonished him and ordered him to get his butt to Orlando, pronto. He arrived that evening just in time for the Magic's next game.

NOTE TO SHAQ: I was shocked by the recent revelation that when L.A. Lakers' teammate Kobe Bryant accused you of being "fat and lazy," you allegedly ramped up the feud between you two by threatening to kill him. Therefore, I just want to go on record that I had nothing to do with this chapter about you. I think a playful editor at the publishing house, no doubt a Kobe fan, must have written it and slipped it into this book. Honest, Shaq. – L.G.

ACTUALLY, THE title of biggest man-child in basketball didn't belong solely to Shaq. It was probably a tie with the Magic's center/forward Stanley Roberts, who also had been Shaq's college teammate at LSU for two seasons. When Orlando picked Roberts in the first round of the 1991 NBA draft – a year before the Magic would acquire O'Neal -- Roberts was 7 foot, 285 pounds. A pleasant, unassuming lad with a disarming smile, Roberts was not as talented or driven as O'Neal. In truth, he probably wasn't all that fired up to be wading hip-deep in humanity as a pro basketball player in the first place. But there was little else he could do back home in his tiny South Carolina hometown to earn three million dollars a year.

Except for his size, here was a normal, engaging young man trapped in a basketball body – albeit a body that kept expanding. Stanley, you see, loved to eat. He soon became the butt of cruel fat jokes.

To wit: Stanley Roberts is the first NBA player who had to let out his shower curtain . . . Stanley Roberts stepped on the scales and a card came out saying, "Come back when you're alone." . . . Stanley Roberts spent Thanksgiving floating over the Macy's parade.

Yuk, yuk, yuk. But it wasn't so funny to the Orlando Magic. Alarmed by his weight gain early in his first year with the Magic, team officials came up with an expensive plan designed to keep him from tilting the gym each time he walked in. They hired a lady nutritionist to buy his food and plan his meals, and a chef to actually go to Stanley's home every day to turn those carefully selected groceries into healthy, weight-conscious lunches and dinners at something far south of 25,000 calories.

After a month of this, team officials weighed Stanley and were shocked to discover he had lost only one pound. *One*. Time for the moment of truth. They turned the thumb screws on him demanding to know why his specially-prepared diet wasn't slimming his considerable silhouette.

"Those things that nice lady has been giving me tasted okay," he nodded, adding sheepishly, "but every few days I had to go out and get me a 10-piece bucket!"

He quickly ballooned to more than 300 pounds and could run up and down the court only in brief stints. The Magic figured they had to either let him go or install an oxygen tank in the bench area. Other teams took turns giving Stanley a shot. Magic Coach Matt Guokas understood. Basketball coaches' eyes gloss over and they toss all other considerations aside when they have a chance to acquire any breathing seven-footer. "It's irresistible," Guokas explained to me.

The Los Angeles Clippers were one of the teams to give Roberts another shot. But he injured a foot late in the prior season and did little or no exercising in the off-season, except to paint racing stripes on his fork. Shortly before the Clippers were to start pre-season camp, Roberts was discovered to be punishing the scales so far over 300 pounds neither Roberts nor Clippers GM Elgin Baylor would reveal Stanley's precise weight. Baylor, the former Hall of Fame Lakers forward, was livid that Stanley hadn't started serious off-season conditioning as his foot healed. And Baylor wasn't buying Stanley's claim there was nothing he could do to prepare himself for the Clippers' season. The team trainer pointed out that even when Stanley's foot was still tender, he could have swam, worked out on a stationary bike or do pushing exercises – as in pushing away from the table.

"To say he couldn't do anything all summer . . . ," Baylor snorted, shaking his head. "Obviously he could eat!"

The Clippers sent Roberts cross-country to the Duke University weight clinic in North Carolina, but he returned to L.A. still looking like a very tall Fat Albert, a guy who literally ate himself out of the NBA. Must have been a Kentucky Fried Chicken place near the Duke campus.

Chapter 4 -- Payne Stewart, Ben Smith

IN THE YEARS before that mesmerizing airplane mishap took him from us in 1999 on worldwide live TV coverage, PAYNE STEWART came to be fondly embraced by the golf world and beyond for his three major victories, his amusing knickered tournament uniform, his beaming smile and infectious staccato laugh. The two-time U.S. Open winner became golf's beloved court jester, spreading smiles throughout the sport and beyond.

In high school back in Springfield, Missouri, he was a 4-sport letterman and developed the athletic self-confidence that he could win not only in golf, but in most any sporting competition. He underscored that at the Ryder Cup one year when he became the unofficial ping-pong champ in the U.S. team room.

Then the bubble burst one night outside Valdosta, Georgia, during a three-day autumn hunting trip with several Orlando buddies. The buddies were commercial pool builder Butch Von Weller, insurance exec Tom "Catfish" McCoy, realtor and former college football coach John Shelton, and comical auto dealer Ben Smith. A rotund former college halfback. Smith is known for his instant and hilarious one-liners.

Overconfident, Payne had only one box of shotgun shells when Shelton picked him up for the trip. Shelton warned that he would need more ammo, but Payne allowed as how he was such a crack shot he wouldn't need many to bag his limit. Shelton wound up lending Payne a couple more boxes and reported that Payne proved to be little threat to the birds flying south for the winter.

Smith had invited an old friend, Valdosta State football coach Mike Cavan, to share dinner with the group their first night in the south Georgia county that had not relaxed its alcohol restrictions at that time. After dinner, Payne suggested he wanted to go somewhere they could have a few beers before turning in. Cavan said the only option was a rural road house just across the county line, gave directions and tried to excuse himself. Payne and Smith talked him into joining the late-night beer jaunt.

Cavan had been an assistant coach at the University of Georgia, renowned as the man who recruited legendary Herschel Walker to become a Bulldog. He had spent several years traveling the Georgia backroads hunting football prospects and knew of the clientele that hung out at the raucous road houses. Predictably, this road house was surrounded by pickup trucks, several with Confederate flags and shotguns on display in the rear window racks. The visiting bird hunters ordered their first round of beers and, perched atop bar stools, became enthralled by a spirited pool game in progress among the good ol' boys. After another round of beers and assessing the action on the nearby pool table, Payne whispered to Cavan: "I think you and I could beat these guys."

From experience, Cavan knew one must have his billiards A-game to take on most of the regulars at such rural Georgia establishments. He cautioned Payne, but to no avail. Within moments, Payne and the reluctant Cavan took on the winners of a just-ended game.

Playing "Eight ball," things went nicely in the first couple of games as the visitors scored narrow victories to win modest bets. Then the good old boys asked to raise the stakes. OK with Payne.

Cavan rolled his eyes, knowing what was coming: The first two games had been bait to suck in the visitors for the rout that was to follow. Suddenly, the home team began running pool balls into pockets like frightened field mice. Payne refused to back down, assuring Cavan he would cover the ever-increasing bets. But the locals ran off a string of high-stakes victories. "Time to go," Cavan finally insisted.

Smith, the funny car dealer, put a sniggering epitath on the ill-fated competition: "When Payne left that place, it looked like an elephant had stepped on his wallet!"

It was just one of hundreds of hilarious one-liners Smith was known to produce. He regularly supplied me with late-model cars at a huge discount. My wife wanted to trade in her little BMW after it cost us large and frequent maintenance bills. "Oh, Mary," Smith lamented. "I'd rather have a fist full of bus tickets than a Beamer!" He took it on trade for a new Toyota.

Another time, when I drove my car to his dealership to pick up a newer one that Smith had picked out for me, he was busy trying to close a sale with a woman interested in a very small Toyota pickup. She wanted to attach a bumper hitch to accommodate a boat or trailer of some sort and questioned if the little Toyota had sufficient power to pull the load.

"M'am," chortled Smith, "that Toyota truck can pull a fat lady out of a donut shop!"

Ben laughed. The lady laughed. She grabbed the papers and signed the deal.

ALTHOUGH HE WAS not a sports icon on Payne's level, Smith was known as an outstanding football player. He led Valdosta High to a couple of Georgia school boy championships under legendary coach Wright Bazemore. He was recruited by another coaching legend, Bobby Dodd, to play at Georgia Tech where he teamed with an old high school teammate of mine, All-SEC linebacker Harold "Swede" Ericksen.

Many years later, Ericksen was one of the surprise roasters when several of us ambushed Smith on his 50th birthday. Because he was popular among southern football figures, Smith's roasters included such prominent names as Auburn coach Pat Dye and Florida State coach Bobby Bowden in live or videotaped jabs. Ericksen's was the topper.

"I'm glad that Ben and Betty were able to have healthy children," Ericksen began. "I worried a lot about that after what happened when they were married. Most of the Tech team was there and after the wedding, we held Ben down behind the church and locked his testicles in a bicycle lock!"

The laughter was uproarious. And when all the playful insults and barbs were exhausted, Ben rose to the podium, almost speechless. Almost.

"There have been a lot of lies told here tonight," he began through a grin. "But Swede's story about the bicycle lock is true. And it just about *white-eyed* me to get the danged thing off!"

More of Ben Smith jocular philosophy: Ben and I and wives attended the posh Pro-Am Awards Dinner on the eve of the PGA Tour's Arnold Palmer Invitational at Bay Hill Club, which each year featured a name performer to entertain the upscale audience. This particular year, the headliners were The Judds, Winona and Naomi. The mother-daughter team were country music favorites, but this upper crust audience was more into the likes of Barbra Streisand or Dionne Warwick. As the Judds' after-dinner performance progressed the audience rapidly thinned out. After about three songs – all of which sounded the same to his ear -- Ben announced he was ready to join the exodus. As we pulled away from the banquet hall, he declared, "I'll tell you what. The Judds could empty a room faster than a fire alarm!"

Over golf one day, Ben said his wife had given him a hard time that morning. "Betty was jumping around like a Puerto Rican shortstop!"

At the news a certain basketball player landed a multi-million-dollar contract: "He's getting more money than a show dog can jump over!"

I once invited him to play at my home club, Orange Tree Golf Club, where the fairways are notoriously claustrophobic and framed by out-of-bounds markers on both sides of most holes. After four holes, Ben, a low-handicap golfer, had already knocked three drives barely out of bounds.

"Gawwwddam!" he snorted. "This place has more white stakes than Arlington Cemetery!"

He came up with laugh-out-loud quips for most any occasion.

BACK TO PAYNE: Though Payne was a multi-talented athlete, he was not mechanically inclined. After several PGA Tour victories enhanced his financial standing, Payne and his wife upgraded from a golf villa on the 12th hole of Orlando's Bay Hill Club to a 10,000-square-foot manse about three miles south of the club. That put him hard by the shoreline of the expansive Butler chain of lakes. So he bought a new bass fishing boat with a powerful outboard engine that could send him streaking across his new watery playground.

Eager to crank up his new toy, he turned over the ignition switch while the boat was still perched atop a trailer in his garage, oblivious to the fact that outboard engines need to pump lake water through its cooling system to protect the engine. When Payne cranked the engine on the trailer, he liked the roar it made there in the enclosed garage. So he gleefully pumped the throttle, revving it a few times to enjoy the throaty sound. Suddenly, he flinched as the motor exploded. He looked up, horrified, as billows of black smoke and orange flames kissed off the ceiling of the garage. Luckily, fireman Payne managed to put out the four-alarm blaze before he burned down his new mansion.

Sniggering word of the incident quickly spread among the PGA Tour pros. At a tournament soon after, one player taped to Payne's locker a large magazine ad for an outboard motor, over which was scrawled, "Just Add Water!"

TO HIS CREDIT, Payne did perform a rare aquatic feat in his backyard lap pool a few hours after winning Arnold Palmer's Bay Hill Classic in 1987. The victory was something of a welcomed breakthrough after Payne had failed to finish off potential wins. In his prior nine starts, Payne finished second three times shooting pedestrian final rounds of 72 and 71 in the closing rounds of those runnerup disappointments. This time, however, he fired a brilliant 7-under-par 65 to close the deal and a celebration was in order.

Within hours, Payne had assembled some two dozen close friends at that golf villa home for a frolicking good time. At one point, Payne was standing near me and a few others at one end of the little lap pool, which was about 3 or 4 yards wide and about 20 yards long. At the far end was a reel which could let out or reel in a fabric cover that could attach at the other end of the pool. The cover was in place, floating atop the water to keep the heat in and leaves out. Some playful guest wondered aloud if it was possible for a person to walk across the cover from one end to the other.

Payne greeted the inquiry with his trademark staccato laugh. "I'd don't know," he said through an impish smile. "Let's give it a try."

With that, Payne, fully dressed and holding his cocktail high, stepped off onto the pool cover and began high-stepping toward the other end. With each stride, his leg disappeared into the pool cover up to his knee, but he kept churning until he stepped out at the far end without spilling a drop of his drink or dousing his slacks.

The onlookers cheered, much the way they had hours earlier when he putted out on the final green to seal the victory. It was just that kind of day when William Payne Stewart could walk on water.

PAYNE'S SIGNATURE tournament outfit -- the knickers, coordinated high socks, jaunty cap from a bygone era and chrome-tipped flamboyant golf shoes – was an inspiration from his father. Bill Stewart was a traveling furniture salesman best known for his amateur golf conquests and his wardrobe of garish striped and plaid sport coats in blazing colors. Payne and his two sisters were known to gag and protest: "Dad, you're not really going out dressed like THAT, are you!!??" each time Bill was departing for a round of sales calls. Dear ol' dad explained to the kids that it was vital for him to establish an identity that would separate him from all the other furniture salesmen. He wanted clients to remember him and it was hard to forget the slender, upbeat guy who exploded into the showrooms like a starburst.

Years later, Payne was on the practice tee at some PGA Tour event early in his first full rookie season, 1982. He looked left and nearly every player on that side was decked out in red golf slacks and a white golf shirt. Looking right, ditto. Looking in the mirror, ditto. He thought back to his dad's philosophy and pondered several options to make his haberdashery/marketing masterstroke before settling on knickers. Tentatively, he gave it a shot during one round of the Atlanta tour stop.

Unfortunately, he was paired that day with jocular Lee Trevino, the playful needler *cum laude* of the PGA Tour. Warming up on the practice tee, Trevino gravely shook his head at first sight of Payne's look-at-me costume. The Merry Mex proceeded to hammer the needle so deep during their round that Payne – usually unabashed – began feeling self-conscious and more than a bit foolish. Trevino, wisecracking to the gallery surrounding one green, motioned toward Payne and loudly chortled: "I bet you folks thought you were coming to a golf tournament, not a kindergarten fashion show!"

But after the round, Payne was emboldened by compliments from a lady volunteer in the scoring tent, then from a couple of approving fellow pros in the locker room. So golf's budding court jester was encouraged to stay the course – but not again in that Atlanta tournament, lest he would have to endure another eighteen holes of barbs from the relentless Trevino.

Over the years, golf galleries everywhere affirmed that he had made a sound decision. The mere first sight of Payne's amusing garb bouncing into view invariably produced an epidemic of grins in the grandstands scattered around the world's tournament courses. Here comes fun, they seemed to express. And it was instant recognition. Nobody confused him for drones like John Cook or Lee Janzen.

His trademark competitive outfit came with a bonus. When he was home and out of "uniform," he could navigate Orlando with minimal intrusion with which other celebrities have to cope. Dressed in full-length khaki pants and without his jaunty Hogan cap, many observers failed to recognize the major golf champion seated there at the next table or wandering in the produce section of the neighborhood supermarket.

Just days after he won the 1999 U.S. Open at Pinehurst, he accompanied his son and daughter to a nearby Wal-Mart to buy a few things for the kids' approaching summer camp. He passed an elderly couple and noticed in his peripheral vision they were giving him second looks. "Hey, hey. I think that's Payne Stewart," the man told his wife. Payne paused near them, pretending to examine some item on the shelf, but actually listening and watching out of the corner of his eye as the scenario played out.

The woman gave him a thorough inspection. Finally, she turned back to her husband with a sneer, and Payne heard her rejoinder: "Nah-h-h-h. That guy's not Payne Stewart. No way."

THERE WERE actually two Payne Stewarts. Payne 1 was one of those quick-success young athletic stars who are all-too-typically self-absorbed and condescending to fans, reporters, officials, and volunteers. Payne 1, quite simply, was a jerk. Payne 2, who evolved after he matured a bit and experienced a spiritual transformation, was respectful and good-neighborly.

The difference in the two Paynes can be illustrated by his behavior as a spectator at other sports. The first Payne was a mean-spirited boor at his son's Little League games, and especially so at home games of the expansion NBA Orlando Magic. His Magic season tickets were located three rows up right behind the Magic bench. Payne's taunts became so loud and unruly that embarrassed friends avoided sitting with him. Prime target for Payne's heckling was the Magic's first head coach, Matty Guokas, who had to endure the loud, often vicious taunts from just a few feet away. Coaching a young, expansion team can be exasperating enough, but Payne made it a living hell for Guokas.

The next season, the Magic moved Payne's season tickets to the opposite side of the court.

When son Aaron played Little League baseball, Payne was right there in the stands giving the umpires fits. But it was required in one league for a parent representing each team to volunteer as first-base or third-base umpires. Payne understood the ploy. "They knew I couldn't scream at the umpires," Payne admitted, "if I *was* one."

What was incongruous about Payne 1's bellicose heckling was that he played a sport where the participants often melt down if someone so much as jiggled change in their pockets from across three fairways. When Payne 2 emerged, his barbs from the stands went from mean-spirited to fun-spirited. Example: Payne became friends with baseball star Ken Griffey, Jr., who lived and golfed in Orlando between baseball seasons. So Payne and fellow Tour stars Mark O'Meara and John Cook made the trek over to St. Petersburg to see their friend Griffey, whose Seattle Mariners were playing the Tampa Bay Rays. They sat in the centerfield bleachers to be near where Griffey played. At one point in the game, Griffey lost sight of a high fly ball against the background of the stadium's roof. Griffey circled desperately trying to get a bead on the ball and made an unsuccessful last-second lurch for the ball, which fell harmlessly to the turf.

When Griffey returned to his position the next inning, Payne called out, "Hey, Junior! Junior!" Griffey recognized the voice and looked up. "Does this look familiar?" shouted Payne, who began frantically running little circles in the walk space next to his seat, then lurching at an imagined ball to parody what happened the inning earlier. Junior Griffey could only cover his face with his glove to hide the laughter.

THERE WAS NOTHING MUCH funny in the wake of Payne's tragic death in October, 1999, when a rented private jet lost all cabin air shortly after takeoff from Orlando. The pilots, Payne, the top two agents in the small firm that represented him, and a golf course architect all were dead within minutes. On automatic pilot, the little jet kept flying northwesterly across country, watched by worldwide television coverage until it finally ran out of fuel and crashed in a South Dakota prairie.

The world was gripped by a searing heartache when it was confirmed that Stewart was, indeed, aboard.

About the only thing amusing that emerged was the laughable actions by the inexperienced young attorney whom the widow Tracey Stewart embraced to handle her affairs. Let's just call him W. B. Ears (W.B. as in "wet behind ears"), who was little more than a glorified office boy at the firm which managed Payne's endorsements and other business. But with the management firm's top two principals taken out by the plane crash, young Mr. Ears was the only surviving lawyer.

Two things happened the next day. I wrote a column advocating that a major street in Orlando be renamed Payne Stewart Boulevard. And after hearing from several publishing houses (who were aware Payne and I had been talking about collaborating on a book), I shared that with Tracey and offered to include her in whatever capacity she wanted to jointly produce a literary tribute to Payne.

She could be the co-author, write a foreword, whatever, and we'd split the royalties. I suggested that since it would not look right for her to profit from Payne's death, she might want to follow my lead and donate a portion or all of her share of the royalties to his favorite charity.

Tracey hugged me and said, "Talk to my attorney and let's get it done."

But Mr. Ears refused to meet with me, face-to-face, advising by phone that I could be the writer on the condition that ALL royalties would go to Tracey. And if the chosen publisher wanted to pony up "a little extra fee" (his words) for me as the writer, that was okay with him. It turns out that he had convinced Tracey that only she had the right to pen and profit from a book on Payne Stewart – a public figure by any standard.

I declined the generous offer, said I would be proceeding with my own, but would be glad to help whomever they chose to ghost-write a book with Tracey. With his assistance, she sent a letter to many of the top PGA Tour stars asking them to work only with the writer she hired and not cooperate with me. Several of those letters were forwarded to me from players, who asked what this was all about and offered to share with me all of their Payne memories I needed.

A third Payne book, primarily a collection of on-course anecdotes, was produced by Cumberland House in Nashville, where publisher Ron Pitkin told me he was contacted by "some guy" in the Tracey Stewart camp. Pitkin is a former minister and a solid businessman who, years earlier, published a book I wrote with former NCAA champion basketball coach Norm Sloan. "I was asked to hold release of our Payne book for several months ," said Pitkin, "so Tracey could have the Payne book market to herself for awhile." This was tantamount to Gimbels saying they had a bad quarter, so would Macy's mind closing their doors for a few months? Pitkin declined, noting that producing and selling books is the business Cumberland House was in.

But the reaction to the re-naming of a street for Payne was the capper. My column proposing such a tribute drew strong support from Central Floridians who had come to admire and appreciate Payne's considerable involvement in the Orlando area. Mel Martinez, then chairman of the Orange County Commission, was among that number and began taking steps to make Payne Stewart Boulevard happen. Martinez, who was later appointed to George W. Bush's cabinet as HUD Secretary and elected to the U.S.Senate, first had to overcome staff objections over the cost of replacing five miles of road signs and irritating all the businesses that would have to revise their mailing addresses. But Mel persisted.

The chosen street was the over-named Apopka-Vineland Road, a major thoroughfare in southwest Orlando with loads of significance for Payne. It starts near Disney World, where Payne first earned his Tour card in Qualifying School and later won the Walt Disney World Classic. The street meanders north past a side street where Payne's lakefront mansion was located; then past the main entrance to Bay Hill, his home course where he won Arnold Palmer's tournament, then past Bay Hill Village where he lived in that golf villa several years, and finally past the serenely idyllic graveyard where Payne's few remains rest near the edge of a calming lake.

Martinez sent a courtesy letter to Tracey Stewart to inform her of the plan and offered that she would be welcome to participate in the dedication ceremony when the time came. The reply to Martinez was a terse letter from Mr. Ears who declared that Tracey would "agree" to the street re-naming only if Orange County purchased an insurance policy that would indemnify anyone in the Stewart family should someone involved in an accident on the newly-named Payne Stewart Boulevard decide to sue the Stewarts.

W. B. Ears. Funny guy.

That farcical declaration should earn him a place in the Overlawyering Hall of Fame. Imagine all the legal exposure the King family would be battling due to fender-benders on all of the innumerable Martin Luther King Boulevards all over the country. It did, however, earn a white flag of surrender by Martinez. He knew that Tracey and Ears had no legal right to block the project, but he shook his head in disgust and scrapped the whole re-naming plan. What should have become Payne's miles-long strip of asphalt in well-deserved and permanent tribute to him remains Apopka-Vineland Road.

P.S. – My book (*The Payne Stewart Story*) and Tracy's compassionate, well-filtered tome both made several bestseller lists. Pitkin reports that his firm's book also did well.

P.P.S. – I have to admit I did take some solace from the fact that Payne's spunky mother, Bee, volunteered to sit with me during two book-signing appearances in Payne's hometown, Springfield, Mo. A reporter from a local TV station interviewed us and curiously asked Bee why she was so supportive of my book while her daughter-in-law also had a Payne book on the shelves. "That book???" she retorted. "Borrrrr-ing!"

Chapter 5 – Cris Collinsworth

Very early in his highly-visible status as a star wide receiver for the Cincinnati Bengals, gregarious Cris Collinsworth developed an interest in the ponies. He loved to visit one of the Cincinnati-area thoroughbred tracks – either River Downs in Ohio or Turfway Park, just across the river in Florence, Ky. Often with an attractive young lady on the arm of this extremely eligible bachelor, at the time.

(A brainy and striking beauty named Holly later put an end to that status and the couple now have two very handsome sons and a pair of gorgeous daughters and Cris has become a top NFL analyst and commentator for NBC-TV. Collectively, this is the high-profile Family Attractive.)

With his disarming ability to poke fun at himself, Cris happily attracts friends, then and now, and a few of those happened to be horse owners. It came to pass that he eagerly accepted an offer to buy a minor partnership in a spirited, but promising young racehorse. The pony had good bloodlines and Cris was free to embrace the dream of every horse owner – cheering on his steed down the stretch of a future Kentucky Derby.

That dream quickly dissolved out of focus as Yarrastar (" I think that was his name.") finished in the back of the pack in his first couple of starts. Alas, it happened again one sunny day when Cris had brought along a beautiful miss to be squired around the clubhouse and impressed with his lofty owner status as he showed her the VIP areas, the barns and other areas of the track. After the race, the principals – trainer, owners, jockey -- made their way to the barn where their slow-poke horse was stabled. They huddled for a strategy session on how to make the animal more productive. The young lady was still on Cris' arm as a singular option was broached: having the horse gelded.

"Yes, yes!" Cris agreed, with authority in his voice. "I've been thinking that might be the best thing to do in this case." He nodded emphatically to impress the young lady that he was a wise and seasoned horseman.

Then he leaned close to his owner-partner and whispered: "What does that mean – gelded?" The partner whispered back that it means snipping off the horse's testicles.

Collinsworth's eyes became horrified saucers. "B-b-but," he stammered, "shouldn't we WARN him first??!!"

A vision comes to mind: With the animal's bridle in one hand and a pair of menacing clippers in the other, the rookie owner lays down the ominous warning. "Now listen up, nag. One more race out of the money and you see these clippers?. . . "

Years later, Cris laughs in retelling the incident. "It just seemed to me the threat would be a greater motivator than the act. I still think I'm right."

Perhaps so, if and when thoroughbred operations, which are constantly experimenting with bloodline breeding, start cranking out racehorses that understand English.

IN A STUNT for charity in 1993, Collinsworth agreed to actually race a thoroughbred himself, in a sprint at River Downs. The horse was ridden by top female jockey Patricia "P.J." Cooksey. Cris wasn't carrying a jockey, thus giving him the edge he felt would prevail.

Indeed, as "Man vs. Beast" broke from the start, Cris spurted ahead. But then as the horse gathered momentum he began to cut Cris' lead and overtook him to win by a nose at the wire. One wonders if Cris would have been more motivated for the run if Patricia had insisted on a provision that the loser would be gelded.

FORTUNATELY, CRIS rarely lost in a sprint against two-legged opponents – not most NFL players, and especially not in high school back in Titusville, Fla., where he was a schoolboy sprint champion.

Collinsworth is built along the general lines of a Caucasian stork – in sharp contrast to most top high school sprinters who are generally stocky, well-muscled African-Americans. As Cris and his usually all-black competitors went through final stretching at the starting line, he tried to emulate that of the intimidating black persona, as best he could. He strutted and flexed as if to say, "I'm baaad! Yeah, Bro', I'm baaad!!"

Up in the grandstand, brother Greg Collinsworth typically positioned himself in close proximity to parents, older brothers, classmates of the sprinters. Moments before the starter's gun, Greg would wave a small stack of cash and declare for all to hear: "I'm betting on the white guy. Anybody here want to cover me?"

Sketchy track and field records show that Greg's bets were covered in an average of 2.35 seconds. Then the gun would go off and those gangly legs by the white guy gobbled up extended lengths of real estate before Cris hit the tape first and Greg pocketed the bets.

CRIS WAS ASSIGNED by NBC to cover his first Summer Olympics in 1996 in Atlanta. Because he had been a standout track athlete in high school, the network assumed he would be able to handle reporting at that venue. He was given the relatively easy task of conducting brief interviews with featured runners as they came off the track.

In the semifinals of the 100-meter dash, Frankie Fredericks from the small African nation of Namibia, won his heat and barely missed the world record despite pulling up short of the finish line and cruising across knowing he had qualified for the finals. The run was very impressive and the stadium was abuzz over Fredericks' eye-popping time. Cris had no interview with Fredericks, but was scheduled to talk to Dennis Mitchell, an American, after the next heat. Mitchell was favored by many to win the 100-meter gold medal. Mitchell also won his heat, but not in particularly impressive style.

The network's track producers had hammered into Cris to get to the point quickly and pose no fluff questions. So as Mitchell caught his breath after running his heat, Cris asked his fellow Florida Gators grad, "Dennis, do you think you can beat Frankie Fredericks in the final? He nearly set the world record in his heat and basically jogged across the finish line." There was a pregnant pause as Mitchell glared at Collinsworth for what seemed many seconds and walked away with a look of disgust on his face, never uttering a word.

In his ear piece, Cris could hear track anchor Tom Hammond laughing hysterically.

Cris : "Back to you, Tom."

Tom : "There's Cris, once again getting the very best out of these athletes."

What Cris didn't hear or see was that Hammond threw it back to Bob Costas, who was NBC's overall anchor for the Olympic telecast. Costas held up a sheet of blank paper, flipped it over a couple of times and declared: "I was just going over a transcript of Cris Collinsworth's interview with Dennis Mitchell."

Cris recalled the incident as follows: "That brought the house down and nearly my TV career with it."

Fredericks was second in the final for the silver medal and Mitchell finished a disappointing fourth, no doubt preoccupied by how he should have answered Collinsworth.

IN WHAT HE THOUGHT was his final game with the Cincinnati Bengals in 1985, Collinsworth caught a late pass from Boomer Esiason and, as too often happened, was tackled on the one-yard line. Bengals quarterbacks

Esiason and Kenny Anderson often teased Cris that he set NFL records for the most receptions that ended one yard short of the end zone.

Unfortunately, Cris suffered a severe ankle sprain on the play and Bengals trainer Marv Pollens rushed onto the field to tend the fallen star. Was this the way Cris' distinguished career would end, with him writhing in pain there on the ground just short of the goal line? Unhappy with the Bengals' contract talks, Cris had signed a "futures" contract with the Tampa Bay Bandits of the new United States Football League and seemed destined to leave the Bengals to play in the upstart spring league. However, the Bengals would adjust their offer for the next season and Cris would continue his career in Cincinnati.

Pollens gently grabbed Collinsworth's ankle for examination and Cris immediately started screaming and kicking at him. "What is it?" Pollens asked. "What did I do?"

Cris groaned and said, "Marv, you're killing me. That end zone camera is trying to get a good farewell-to-Cris Collinsworth shot, and your big ass is in the way."

Nonplussed, Pollens snapped Collinsworth's ankle to one side and dropped his leg, forcing Cris to limp back to the sideline without the traditional arm over the trainer's shoulder for the proper sendoff this brave soldier so richly deserved.

I FIRST CAME to know Chris when he was a highly recruited freshman quarterback at the University of Florida. At the time, I was the lead sports columnist at the *Orlando Sentinel.* Assuming it would be wise to develop a good working rapport with this kid who was likely to be a major storyline for the next four years, I invited him, during preseason practices, for a dinner interview at one of Gainesville's best restaurants. On my *Sentinel* expense account, of course. It became obvious that Cris would never settle for the mundane; He perused the right side of the menu and ordered surf-and-turf, the most expensive entrée on the menu.

He did, indeed, become a valuable interview after Gator football games in his junior season because he was virtually the *only* interview. Florida struggled through an 0-10-1 season and most of his fellow teammates were reluctant to talk about it. The gregarious Collinsworth became the go-to guy for reporters after each accumulating defeat.

Two years earlier, in his very first game for the Gators, he engraved his name in the NCAA record books with a feat that can be tied, but never topped. Taking the snap at Florida's own one-yard line against Rice, Collinsworth threw to wideout Derrick Gaffney for a 99-yard touchdown. But after spotty success behind center, Cris was shifted to wide receiver, a position where he flourished the rest of his decorated college and pro career.

Somewhere during our relationship, Cris and I embraced a jocular challenge: To see which of us could make it longer through life without ever having a real job. I was a sports writer and Cris was a football player, then highly-paid TV football commentator teamed with Al Michaels. None of those are regarded by the unwashed masses as exercises of bona fide labor.

I won. I took early retirement from the *Sentinel* in 2000 and, as of this writing, Cris is still working. Sort of.

Chapter 6 – Woody Hayes

FOUR YEARS after joining the staff of the *Orlando Sentinel*, I was assigned to cover a much-anticipated 1977 season-opening game between Ohio State's Buckeyes and the Miami Hurricanes at Columbus. My primary objective, however, was not so much the game (won by Ohio State, 10-0), but to gather fodder for an in-depth feature on Ohio State's legendary and controversial throw-back head coach, Woody Hayes.

Well known was that Hayes kept the media at arm's length, allowing limited access to himself, his staff and, most of all, his players. I had a good relationship with Lou Holtz, then head coach at Arkansas, who had served earlier as an assistant coach under the often brusque Hayes. Before I flew to Columbus, Lou made a call to Woody and vouched for me – I guess giving Hayes the assurance I wouldn't physically maim one of his linebackers or reveal to "that school up north" (hated rival Michigan) the intricate secrets of the Buckeyes' relentless 3-yard plunges into the center of the line.

So off I went, several days ahead of the Miami game, to meet the fearsome volcano named Woody. Much to my surprise, Coach Hayes received me cordially, sat for an extremely rare one-on-one interview in his spartan little field house "office" that contained a cot for his daily naps, a small desk and a bookcase crammed with volumes of military history. He even allowed me to watch a practice and one of his informal classes that he personally taught each summer for the benefit of incoming freshman players between pre-season practices. The theme of the unofficial class was a combination of English and history and the objective – as Woody explained – was to make up for the shortcomings of our public education system and better prepare his incoming players for the college classroom challenges they would face in the weeks to come. I came away impressed with Prof. Hayes' skills as an orator. The gathered

18- and 19-year-olds were riveted – as was I -- by Woody's often humorous and ribald anecdotes about the personal lives of historic kings and generals.

He sought to expand their vocabularies with new words each day. The day I was an interloper in the class, the words were "apathy" and "sycophant." Woody warned them to avoid any people who were apathetic or sycophants. "Avoid them like the plague," he said, over and over. Apparently, he was okay with clichés.

During my week on campus, I witnessed an example of his well-known short fuse. The practice observed, the day before the Miami game, was conducted in the massive Ohio Stadium. There were several rows of folding chairs behind the bench area and in front of the regular seats in anticipation of an overflow crowd the next day. As the first team ran through selected plays, some of the scrubs chilled out in the folding chairs. Hayes looked over to discover this affront to mankind and erupted. He ran screaming toward the lounging scrubs, commanding them to "get off your asses and pay attention to the plays!" The young players scattered like startled fawns and Hayes began slinging a dozen or more of the folding chairs up into the permanent seats.

Widely known, of course, is that Woody's legendary tenure as the Buckeyes coach later came to an infamous end days after he punched a Clemson linebacker who had chased one of his Buckeye runners into the Ohio State bench area during the Gator Bowl.

A FEW WEEKS after Woody was fired, I had the good fortune to break the national story that Iowa State coach Earle Bruce – a former Woody assistant – was about to be named as the new Ohio State coach. I called another prominent coach who had been interviewed for the job and had just been told by Ohio State officials that Bruce would be named the next day. The coach was miffed enough that he provided me with the direct phone number to Bruce's office at Iowa State.

To my good fortune, Bruce answered the call as he was cleaning out his desk. Though reluctant at first, Bruce admitted that, yes, he would be introduced the next day as Woody's successor in a press conference in Columbus. My *Orlando Sentinel* breaking story on the eve of that official announcement was picked up by Associated Press late that evening and carried throughout the land.

The next day, after the official press conference, the sports editor of one of Columbus' two daily newspapers called me in Orlando. He was miffed that his paper had been scooped on this important story and pointedly asked how a southern newspaperman all the way down in Florida could have known Bruce had been hired. The guy's tone was haughty and demeaning.

His condescending attitude inspired me to pointedly retort: "Well, we have a marvelous new device down here. It's called a telephone. You can punch in various numbers and talk to people all over the country." The Columbus sports editor was not amused.

THE WEEK I WAS in Columbus for the Buckeyes-Hurricanes game, I was not the only media person given rare access to Woody and his program. British Broadcasting had a crew there, filming a documentary about Hayes. It was part of a BBC series called, "The Americans," which featured varying persons and occupations in the U.S. Producers wanted to include a college football coach. Woody was one of the best-known at that time, but the BBC was warned that he typically kept all media at double arm's length. Nevertheless, they contacted him and he accepted, agreeing that the BBC crew would have unfettered access to everything that week – practices, staff meetings, pregame and halftime locker room, everything.

I met the executive producer of the BBC project and asked why Woody uncharacteristically opened all doors to his camera crew. A short, painfully thin man who could have easily been mistaken for a jockey, the producer said he had wondered the same thing and asked Woody why the uncommon welcome.

"Who was the greatest person in all mankind?" Woody began his explanation.

The producer shrugged and thought for a moment. "Jesus Christ?"

Woody shook his head.

The producer, having picked up on Woody's love of military history, tried that tack. "Napoleon Bonaparte? George Patton?"

Irritated, Woody fired back: "No, you pussy! It was Winston goddam Churchill, that's who! If Churchill hadn't stood up to Hitler, we would all be speaking German now!"

Obviously, Hayes had welcomed the BBC as his personal payback to England for saving our bacon.

IT HADN'T TAKEN long for Lou Holtz to learn how intense Woody could become after young Lou signed on the winter of 1968 to become Woody's defensive secondary coach. In the very first staff meeting Lou attended, Woody expressed his disappointment in the effort he perceived that his staff was making in the off season. He expressed it by hurling a film projector though the glass portion of the door.

"They repaired the door, adding some bars over the glass part and attached a chain to the projector," recalls Holtz. Concerned, he called a former Hayes assistant named Tiger Ellison, who had talked Lou into taking the Ohio State secondary coaching position over a similar offer from Georgia Tech. "You'll get used to it. You'll be glad you came," assured Ellison. "Woody is demanding, but he is fair."

"He was right," Holtz recounts. "My experience at Ohio State was marvelous. Coach Hayes taught me so much about leadership, about people, about fundamentals. He was an incredible individual and the most loyal American, and one of the most well-read men I've ever met."

AFTER ONE SEASON as an assistant coach at Ohio State, in which Lou Holtz was in charge of the defensive secondary and the Buckeyes were undefeated national champs, Lou decided to accept an offer to become head coach at ambitious little William and Mary. He called his intense, legendary boss for permission to come to Woody's home late one evening to break the news. "He unleashed a world record for four-letter words in a 2-minute span," Holtz recalls.

Woody tried to talk his promising young assistant into declining the offer. After he calmed down, Hayes challenged: "Do you really want to be a head coach?"

Lou responded: "I want to find out if I can."

Hayes gave his blessings with conditions: Lou would have to write an extensive paper detailing his pass defense philosophies and tactics, plus help break in his replacement. With those assignments completed and Lou ready to depart, Hayes summoned Holtz back to the coach's modest home. He wrote out a personal check to pay Lou for the paper, but Holtz shoved it back. Irritated, Woody jammed the check into the front pocket of Lou's shirt so hard, he tore the pocket almost completely off the shirt. "And it was my only dress shirt," Holtz recounts with a laugh. "I ripped up the check and he simply started writing another. I told him I could rip up the checks faster than he could write them and I just couldn't accept it."

Years later, Holtz said with a grin he had one regret about that incident. "I didn't see how much he made the check for, so I don't know how much he valued that paper I wrote."

Chapter 7 -- Lou Holtz, Bobby Bowden

The practice of leaving misbehaving star players at home was one that Lou Holtz embraced years later when he was coach at Arkansas. He suspended his top two running backs and best receiver over team infractions as his Razorbacks were preparing for a daunting Orange Bowl challenge against a mighty Oklahoma team that was poised to win its third national title in four seasons.

Always a supreme motivator, Holtz guided his short-handed Razorbacks to an unthinkable 31-6 upset rout over the Sooners. It was perhaps the shining moment in a coaching career in which Holtz became the only college coach to lead six different programs to bowl games and four different programs to final top 20 rankings. He would earn seven different national coach of the year awards.

Holtz had a slight lisp and an unimposing physique, as if Central Casting sent over a bookkeeper instead of a football coach. But Lou is a masterful communicator, who used inspired rhetoric and even magic tricks to motivate and entertain his players. He seemingly could coax a troop of Cub Scouts into taking on a motorcycle gang. Lou was a pattern guy; He was number 001.

ANOTHER STRIKING UPSET VICTORY for Lou came when he was at North Carolina State and his Wolfpack defeated a heavily-favored, defensive-dominant Maryland team coached by Jerry Claiborne,who had been an assistant years earlier under Bear Bryant at Kentucky. The game was being televised and Holtz figured his best shot at scoring was through special teams play. So he chose to have his special teams introduced, rather than the offense or defense as is the norm. His inspired special teams play that day turned out to be the difference.

With an open date the following week, Holtz accepted a dual speaking engagement at the Birmingham and Tuscaloosa quarterback clubs. In Tuscaloosa, it was arranged for him to spend some time in that famed coaching tower with Bryant during a Crimson Tide practice. The old master asked, "How did you beat my boy Jerry Claiborne on Saturday?" Lou explained his tactic of pumping up his special teams by having them introduced on TV just before kickoff.

Later that week, Alabama would be playing an epic SEC matchup with powerful Tennessee. Bryant chose his special teams for pregame TV introductions, which was noted in a *Sports Illustrated* cover-story account of the Alabama victory. "Only Bear Bryant would be smart enough to introduce his special teams," the story proclaimed. When the magazine came out, Bryant called Holtz and apologized for the misplaced credit. Further, he invited Lou to come to Tuscaloosa to speak at his personal coaching clinic the following summer. "He said he would pay me $2,500 in cash," recalls Holtz. Still a young head coach with four children, Holtz said that was big money to him in the mid-70s. The bonus was staying at Bryant's home for three days and further picking the great coach's brain.

"I'll tell you who loved Coach Bryant was Woody Hayes. Woody thought he was the best coach, ever," Holtz says.

A GIFTED SPEAKER, Holtz was a natural for the 10-year run he recently ended as an ESPN college football commentator. That began, he intones, as something of an accident. ESPN had a 3-man panel in place to preview and analyze college games on the same weekend Holtz made a cameo appearance on one of the lesser ESPN shows that Friday. However, one of three college football commentators, Trev Alberts, was suddenly dismissed, leaving the middle chair open. Holtz was asked to stay an extra day and fill in, between former college and pro players Mark May and Reece Davis until the network could hire a replacement the following week.

"There was no script and no teleprompters," Lou recalls. The two regulars carried the show and Lou chimed in now and then. But he got his dander up when May threw a coach under the bus while analyzing a game played that day.

Remembers Lou: "I thought, 'I can't let him get away with that.'" So Lou jumped in and emphatically countered most of May's negative assertions about the particular coach. ESPN officials perked up, quickly signed Holtz to a contract and a vibrant, decade-long yen and yang of Holtz/May was launched. Also a close friendship, despite their opposing points of view.

"Mark is a true professional. I enjoyed working with him. With no script, it was great for me, mentally. I'm probably as sharp today as I was thirty years ago," Holtz says. "Mark was a player; I was a coach. He made suggestions; I made decisions. He signed a paycheck on the back; I signed on the front. But I always had great respect for Mark and still do today. He's a wonderful guy."

After the 2014 season, ESPN broke up the 3-man team. May was moved to ABC, Davis to Game Day and Holtz "retired" to continue as a captivating and popular speaker several times each month.

AFTER SEVERAL YEARS with ESPN, Lou felt the need to get into politics. The Central Florida district in which he and wife Beth reside was represented in Congress by a female Democrat whom he considered inept. Lou entertained the notion of running against that incumbent in the 2012 elections.

"I just became worried about the direction of the country and the turmoil. But rather than complain, maybe I ought to try to go do something about it. At my age at that time, I thought that may be the most productive way I could help. I had so many people urging me to run and guaranteed the money that I would need to run," recalls Lou, who knew he would have to resign from his ESPN commentary position.

The choice was made for him when the local Republican Party chairman, Lew Oliver, foolishly dissed the notion of Holtz running for Congress. "Nobody knows him," was the chairman's remarkable reaction. "He's no Don Shula, you know."

Wounded by the baseless comment, Holtz discarded the notion of running.

Ranking Republicans, aware of Lou's high visibility and speaking skills, felt he would have been a slam-dunk winner of that U.S. House seat. Two years later, in the run-up to the 2014 elections, Georgia congressman Tom Price headed an effort to convince Holtz to run for the U.S. Senate seat held by incumbent Democrat Bill Nelson, who was a rubber-stamp vote for all Obama policies and helped run up the national debt with countless earmark grants to Florida groups in an obvious scheme to buy votes with taxpayer money. (All the while hypocritically speaking on the floor of the Senate in favor of fiscal reform.)

Holtz said he was tempted, but decided against it after talking to former Nebraska football coach Tom Osborne, who served a term in the U.S. House of Representative after retiring from coaching.

"Tom told me, 'You get frustrated. Things work so slowly. You think you can go make a difference, but you really can't.' Between that and having to give up the TV work, that probably had as much to do with me not running as anything."

Holtz said his temptation to enter politics stemmed from the fact he was a history major, a former Army officer and visited troops in the mountains of Afghanistan to observe the Mid-East turmoil.

"I was born with a silver spoon," said Holtz. "And I say that because my dad went only to the third grade. I was born during the Depression. I was born in the cellar, not the hospital. We had one bedroom for my sister, myself and my parents. No closets. A kitchen and a half bath. No refrigerator. I lived there for seven and a half years. There was no welfare, no food stamps.

"But the reason I say I was born with a silver spoon in my mouth is that I was born in this country and I was taught to be responsible for the actions I made. I was taught if I was willing to work and make sacrifices, I could be successful. I had a silver spoon not because of what I had, but what I was taught. I grew up with a love for this country and I still have it."

FLORIDA STATE ICON BOBBY BOWDEN and Lou Holtz have long had a close friendship that started back when they were little-known, but ambitious young coaches. They first met when Bobby was the head coach at Birmingham's tiny Howard College (now Samford University) and Holtz was a graduate assistant at Iowa. As low man on the staff, Lou was assigned the duty of entertaining and transporting any visiting coaches.

Bowden was one of the visitors, along with Canadian Football League coach Bud Grant – later the successful coach of the Minnesota Vikings – and William & Mary coach Milt Drury. Holtz took them to dinner at a place owned by a famous former Yankees pitcher, whose restaurant was known for its exceptionally well-stocked wine cellar.

Holtz and Bowden didn't drink, and thus declined the owner's offer of a complimentary bottle of wine as they departed. Grant and Drury accepted and it was one of those bottles that was dropped and burst all over the floor of the university car that Holtz was allowed to use that evening. Holtz kept the car for a week, afraid to turn it in until the wine odor finally dissipated.

A year later, Bobby's underdog Howard team upset Furman, a game witnessed by Holtz, by then an assistant coach scouting for William & Mary for its approaching game against Furman. Holtz called Bowden the next day to collect all the inside info he could about how little Howard

College pulled off the upset. There was an unusual play in the closing minutes of that game that both coaches remember to this day. On fourth-down at the Furman 17, Bowden decided not to use his inconsistent placekicker and instead pooch punted to the Furman 4.

Holtz: "At Florida State, Bobby became known for his razzle-dazzle offenses. But I always remember him as the guy who once punted from the other team's 17-yard line."

Bowden explains the ultra-conservative ploy thusly: "We had a 7-point lead and we had a good defense. So I decided we would try to back 'em up more and hope we could hold 'em. And we did." Lou's scouting report for his own head coach didn't include the advice of punting from the enemy 17.

When Holtz later became head coach at William & Mary and Bowden had become head coach at West Virginia, they played and Bowden's Mountaineers were heavily favored. Lou's underdogs put up a decent fight, but trailed 28-14 late in the fourth period. It turned into a 42-14 rout when Bowden's team ran for two touchdowns in the closing minutes.

Meeting at midfield after the final horn, Holtz pointedly asked Bowden, "Why did you run the score up?"

"That's your obligation to hold the score down, not mine," Bowden countered. "Either coach harder or recruit better."

Recalling the incident, Bowden said he was taken aback by how angry Holtz was during that midfield meeting. "Lou is very competitive, but I couldn't get over how angry he was. To that point, I had thought of Lou as a nice, funny guy. But he has some toughness about him and there at midfield after that game, I thought he was wanting to *fight*."

Holtz says he never forgot the exchange and adopted Bobby's philosophy when other coaches intimated that Lou had run up the score. A few years later, after Holtz became coach at North Carolina State, his Wolfpack defeated Bowden's West Virginia team 49-13 in the Peach Bowl.

Bowden's usual handling of late-game leads was fomented in a game against Pitt when he was the first-year head coach at West Virginia. "I had been the coach at small colleges to that point, but now I'm coaching at a major program where you are more subject to criticism from the fans and the media," Bowden recounts. The game was at Pitt, West Virginia's main rival, and Bowden enjoyed a 35-8 lead at halftime. "We were wearing them out. Everything we did turned into a touchdown. We adopted a philosophy that if we toned down our offense and just didn't make mistakes in the second half, we had the game won. They come out the second half and beat us, 36-35. That was the darkest day of my coaching career. That influenced my coaching. I never sat on the ball again."

"Bobby is one class act. Never changes. Great with people," Holtz says of Bowden. When the exceptional but troubled receiver Randy Moss was dismissed by Notre Dame, Holtz was the head coach there and Bowden had moved on to Florida State. Holtz met with Randy and his mother and recommended he transfer to Florida State. "I felt the person who handled great athletes better than anyone was Bobby Bowden. He's a great person."

PROMINENT FOOTBALL COACHES have been guilty from time to time of forgetting some player who had already graduated and was no longer available to be sent into a game. Bobby Bowden's "missing" soul was a little closer to home. While an assistant coach at Florida State in 1963, Bowden packed up the family early Christmas morning and embarked on their annual jaunt from Tallahassee to Birmingham where both sets of grandparents lived. At the time, Bobby and wife Ann had six children, ages 3 to 13. They all piled into the family station wagon and made a stop for breakfast in Prattsville, Alabama, before continuing to Birmingham.

After proceeding about 30 miles, the flashing lights of an Alabama Highway Patrol trooper appeared in Bobby's rear-view mirror and he pulled off to the edge of the road. "I didn't think I was speeding, was I?" Bobby asked when the trooper leaned into his window.

"No, but have you left something?" asked the trooper.

"We looked around and starting counting the kids. Our youngest, Ginger, 3, wasn't in the car," Bowden recounts. Ann began crying, fearful of what might have happened to the tyke. Bobby turned the car around, went back to the café and discovered little Ginger sitting up on the counter, having a grand time as waitresses entertained her and plied her with candy.

"Ann gave me heck about that," says Bowden.

YEARS LATER, as a successful head coach at FSU, Bowden was known for his dapper appearance. Except in the offseason when there was any period of time when he didn't have to go the office or appear in public. He would typically dive into one of his countless military history books and lounge around home reading in a ragged old sweatshirt, not bothering to wear shoes, shave or comb his hair for days.

"If I don't have to speak or go anywhere for a few days, I just lounge around," he explained.

During one of these periods, there came a knock at the door when he was home alone. It was the wife of one of his assistant coaches, delivering something or other. When Bowden opened the door, the lady was at a loss for words. The scruffy old guy before her seemed vaguely familiar, but nothing like the head coach she was accustomed to seeing. "Uh-h-h, is Coach Bowden here?" she stammered.

Bobby blinked and called her name. "What do you mean? I *am* Coach Bowden," he said.

BOWDEN's first head coaching job was at South Georgia College, a 2-year school located in Douglas, Ga. He was athletic director, head coach for football and head coach for basketball, the latter a sport for which Bowden readily admits he was not well-versed. His basketball team went 1-15. His football team, however, won the Georgia junior college championship.

The next year, Bowden hired an old high school pal and Howard teammate, Vince Gibson, as his main football assistant. Gibson was a high school assistant coach at the time in St. Augustine, Florida, and agreed to talk to Bobby about joining him at South Georgia. Bobby drove down to talk to Gibson, but ran into a slight problem. At a toll bridge near the Georgia-Florida line, Bowden discovered he had no money on him. He had to back track and drive an extra 30 miles to bypass the toll bridge en route to St. Augustine. Gibson accepted the job, but Bowden, in his role as athletic director, fired himself as basketball coach and saddled Gibson with that extra duty. (Much later, Gibson would become head football coach at Kansas State and Tulane.)

After leaving South Georgia, Bowden and Gibson were fellow assistant coaches at Florida State, on the staff of colorful Bill Peterson. On the same weekend, they were sent to North Carolina to scout two teams coming up on FSU's schedule. Bowden's assignment was North Carolina State, which was hosting Virginia. Gibson was there to study Wake Forest, which was playing at North Carolina. One was a day game, the other at night, and only a few miles apart. So they decided to attend both games together to help one another with their assignments.

They had flown into the Raleigh/Durham airport early that morning and were booked to fly out early the next morning. But the local area hotels were crammed with visiting teams and fans and Bowden recalls they had trouble booking a room. They managed to rent a single hotel room that had only one bed.

"We didn't care. By then, it was near midnight and we could hardly keep our eyes open," Bowden recalls. "In the middle of the night, I woke up to discover Vince had his arms around me, and I had mine around him! We woke up and laughed and laughed and laughed."

Bowden says he slept the rest of that night "with one eye open!"

YEARS LATER, when Bowden was at the height of his celebrated career as Florida State head coach, he encountered Peterson, his former boss, in an exasperating incident in New Orleans. Peterson had become athletic director at Central Florida and his ambitious football team was scheduled to play at Nichols State, not far from New Orleans. On the same Saturday, Bowden's FSU team would be playing Tulane in the New Orleans Superdome.

When the FSU team charter landed at Moisant Airport in New Orleans, they discovered their chartered buses had been commandeered an hour earlier by Peterson and the UCF football team. When UCF had landed, they were asked if they were "the team from Florida." Peterson nodded in the affirmative and the UCF Knights were loaded on the buses intended for FSU. As per instructions, the bus drivers delivered the UCF team to the hotel booked by FSU. Peterson's Knights took not only the FSU hotel rooms, but the private team dining room and team meeting room reserved for FSU. Bowden was livid.

"We had to hang out at the airport for more than an hour while the bus company rounded up replacement buses," Bowden recounts. "Then there was a big wreck on the expressway into downtown and we were stuck there an extra hour." One can only image how happy Bowden was when the team finally reached their intended hotel only to be told the "other Florida team" had FSU's accommodations. While the team sat in the lobby – many of them on the floor – the hotel managed to shift enough reservations to make rooms available for the FSU team, although many of the players had to sleep on extra cots.

"With the private dining room in use, our players had to eat in the public restaurant anywhere they could find a table among the fans and public. An alternative meeting room was made available, albeit one too small for the usual breakout of offense and defense units.

The next time they met, the fun-loving Peterson laughed about the situation. Bowden didn't laugh. To make matters worse, FSU was upset that night by the decidedly underdog Tulane team. Later, the Tulane victory was nullified because the Green Wave had used an ineligible quarterback. But that was little salve for Bowden.

Chapter 8 – Joe Namath, Larry Grantham, Steve Sloan

I first met and had personal interaction with Joe Namath in the early '70s during the times I went to New York late in the football season to visit my old friend and golf-mate, Larry Grantham, the undersized and five-time All-AFL linebacker for the New York Jets. Larry and I grew up in Mississippi, me on the Gulf Coast and Larry in the small town of Crystal Springs about 30 miles south of Jackson.

Larry was a wide receiver at Ole Miss, but was judged too slow to play that position in pro ball, even in the newly-formed American Football League after the Jets drafted him. He was shifted to defensive back, then was moved up one week to fill in for an injured teammate at outside linebacker. There he stayed for the rest of his distinguished career. Although he was officially listed at 210 pounds, Larry said he never topped 192 during his career and often finished off each season barely above 180. He made up for the lack of heft with a pulsing competitiveness and on-field savvy that made him something of the quarterback on the Jets' defense. He was a key component in the Jets' AFL championship season and unthinkable upset victory over the rival NFL Baltimore Colts in Super Bowl III.

After his playing days were over, he fought alcoholism and throat cancer, but never abandoned his fun-loving spirit. He loved to entertain with off-the-field stories about Namath and other teammates. The funniest of those centered on fellow Mississippian Verlon Biggs, a hulking defensive end from the tiny coastal town of Moss Point, who played collegiately at predominantly-black Jackson State.

Verlon was a physical wonder, but mentally – well -- he was never mistaken for a Rhodes Scholar candidate. In one off-season, Biggs bought a small parcel of frontage on Highway 90 near Moss Point and built a night club that had only one parking spot – reserved for Verlon. He assumed his patrons would simply park along the shoulder of Highway 90. But when he showed up for opening night, the highway was flanked with dozens of Department of Transportation signs noting that parking on the shoulder of the highway was a no-no that carried a hefty fine. Biggs had to return to the man who sold him the property to buy a second parcel of land for parking – at a huge premium.

Biggs was the star of Grantham's funniest story about the Jets locker room. The Jets of that era typically took Mondays off (usually to play golf in frigid temperatures, as I discovered during one of my teeth-chattering sleepovers at the Granthams' apartment) then reconvening on Tuesday mornings to begin preparations for the next game.

But Biggs' assignment one Monday was to take his roomie – whom we'll simply call "Mike" for our purposes here – to get checked out by a neurosurgeon after having been kicked in the head during the previous day's game. For Verlon, the highly technical information the doctor offered and the sobering sight of electrodes attached to Mike's head, leading to a pulsing machine, was just enough input to be dangerous. The words "brain" and "surgery" overwhelmed all other information from the doctor who decided to keep Mike overnight for observation.

The next morning, when the team gathered in a meeting room to go over the previous game and begin absorbing facets of the game plan ahead, cherubic head coach Weeb Ewbank paused his presentation at the chalkboard when he noticed Mike was missing.

"Verlon," said Ewbank, "did you take your roomie to the doctor yesterday?"

"Yeah, Coach."

"What did he say?"

Biggs stood and nervously cleared his throat, shifting from one foot to the other. Players began to smile and snicker, anticipating a memorable report. It was more than memorable.

"The doctor," Biggs began, "said they were keeping him overnight to do brain surgery. But he'll be back to practice tomorrow!"

The room erupted with laughter. Grantham recounted that Ewbank collapsed onto a folding chair, his laughter shaking his ample belly, and he thought Namath was going to run out of breath he was laughing so hard.

The first time I heard Grantham tell the story, I suspected it was merely an embellished banquet yarn. He insisted it was factual. Years later, I was paired with Namath in a Celebrity Golf Association tournament in Orlando and ran the story by the iconic quarterback. Joe squinted, obviously pulling up the incident from his memory banks. Then he simply smiled and limped to the next tee box without saying a word.

More recently, after Grantham died, I contacted lineman Paul Rochester at his home in Jacksonville. Rochester was Grantham's road-game roommate during their time with the Jets. Asked if the "brain surgery" story was true, Rochester said: "We all loved Verlon and Larry and I both attended his funeral in Moss Point."

And the brain surgery tale? "It happened," said Rochester.

STEVE SLOAN was a young defensive back at Alabama when he wasn't filling in at quarterback on those occasions when his famous road-game roommate, Joe Willie Namath, was sidelined by knee injuries or disciplinary action from Coach Bear Bryant. As the "back-up" quarterback, Sloan was under center when Alabama won two Associated Press national championships in '64 and '65. He became full-time starter the next season when Namath was as rookie with the Jets.

Near the end of the '63 season, Bryant had benched Namath for partaking in one glass of something stronger than ginger ale and Sloan, until then a defensive back, filled in at quarterback for the final regular season game against Miami and in the Sugar Bowl against Ole Miss. "I hadn't played quarterback until then and the quarterbacks back then called their own plays. I hardly knew what I was doing," Sloan modestly recounts. He must have known something; Bama won both games.

By today's standards, a glass of barley and hops would merit little more than an extra lap after practice. Although Sloan roomed with Namath on road games, he said they never discussed the suspension. "I didn't ask and Joe didn't offer anything," Sloan recalls. "We could hardly understand each other, anyway, me being from Tennessee and Joe from Pennsylvania." The coach and the suspended star distinguished themselves with the way they handled the suspension. Bryant demonstrated that he wouldn't compromise his team rules even for a player of Namath's caliber, and Joe accepted the suspension quietly and gracefully. He even stayed at Bryant's house for a couple of days to avoid the media storm.

Chapter 9 – Steve Spurrier, Peyton Manning

Earlier in this book -- in the chapter focusing on Bear Bryant -- was a salute to several sports icons for their rare ability to avoid holding grudges against those who may have angered them with some annoying action. You won't find Steve Spurrier, the contentious, self-absorbed college football coach on that list.

In fact, I would rank "Darth Visor" – as I often referred to him in print -- right up there alongside President Barack Obama among the all-Galaxy grudge holders and narcissists. Their pictures should be in the dictionary alongside the definition of narcissism.

During a recent season in his reign as "head ball coach" at South Carolina, Spurrier erupted over something Columbia newspaper columnist Ron Morris wrote referring to Spurrier's alleged role in talking an athlete into skipping out on the school's basketball team to instead play football. The coach tried, unsuccessfully, to get Morris fired from his newspaper, but he did kick up such a fuss that Morris had to give up his weekly sports show on one of the local TV stations. When he couldn't get the newspaper to fire Morris, Spurrier declared he would not speak to Morris again and noted that he had used that Greta Garbo punishment years earlier on Larry Guest. Me. He named me in a press conference.

Friends and writers called me to ask what that was all about. I had to mentally review the number of years that had passed since Spurrier blew up over a three-sentence item in my weekly notes column in the *Orlando Sentinel*. Three sentences that were affirmed as accurate.

Seventeen. It had been 17 years since that summer when Spurrier demanded I retract the three sentences, "or I will never talk to you again."

Now, during the Morris dustup, he was revealing that he was still livid about my affront to his regal standing. For 17 years, he had been tightly clutching that grudge. Probably still is.

The three sentences came in reference to Spurrier's speaking engagement at the Jacksonville Gator Club, a regular gathering of loyal Florida Gator boosters. It came just a few days before 1993 preseason practice and at a time when Jacksonville civic leaders and politicians were attempting to land a National Football League franchise. On the day of the Gator Club meeting, Jacksonville Mayor Ed Austin announced that he felt the NFL was using Jacksonville only as a negotiating chip to sweeten a deal with St. Louis. Thus, the mayor declared that Jacksonville was withdrawing its bid.

Many of the football diehards in Jacksonville were angered by the mayor's declaration and many of those were in the audience that evening when Spurrier spoke. They still loved the Florida Gators and remained supportive of Spurrier, but they were upset when the Ball Coach, who was known to regularly make caustic, inflammatory comments, said he supported the mayor's move. A few in the audience even booed. Obviously, Spurrier had a dog in this hunt; Jacksonville was a Gator booster stronghold and the coach wasn't eager to share the town with some attention-hogging NFL team.

A friend tipped me the next day and I checked with a Jacksonville reporter whom I suspected would have been at the meeting. He affirmed that some had booed Spurrier's remarks. So in my weekly "three dot" column – a collection of short slants on the sports world -- I wrote the following: *"You can tell football season is almost here because Steve Spurrier put his foot in his mouth at a Jacksonville Gator Club. He expressed support for his friend, Mayor Austin, for withdrawing the city's NFL pursuit. Several in the audience booed."*

By noon on the day that was published, Spurrier angrily phoned me to claim no one there had booed and demanded I write an apology and retraction to appear in the very next day's edition of the *Sentinel*. I confessed that I occasionally erred or had bad information and that I would investigate this alleged travesty of journalism to get to the facts. If I had been misinformed, I said, I would gladly run a correction in my three-dot column the next week.

Wasn't good enough. He wanted a correction and apology NOW.

I called another friend in Jacksonville, Dr. Waylon Coppedge, an avid Gator fan. I knew the good doctor because he was a close pal with Arnold Palmer, whose long-running rule as King of Golf I covered extensively. Waylon said, yes, he was at the Gator Club and, yes, there was some booing at Spurrier's unwelcome remark regarding the NFL pullout. "The guy next to me REALLY booed," he said. "Listen, we still love the Gators and Spurrier, but he was out of line about the NFL thing. We're all mad at the mayor, not Spurrier."

I called Spurrier at his office at UF and reported the results of my fact-checking. I said I wouldn't be writing a correction since the original item turned out to be correct. That's when he told me he would never talk to me again. But he did write. The coach, the son of a minister, penned one of his many legendary, infamous hand-written, obscenity-laced love letters he often mailed to journalists whom he thought should have been drowned at birth. Those would include any misguided writers who were not shameless cheerleaders for him and his football program.

Several of us ink-stained wretches faxed one another copies of these epic letters. Recipients included Dave Hyde of the Fort Lauderdale *Sun-Sentinel*, Mark Bradley of the *Atlanta Journal-Constitution* and Gerald Ensley of the *Tallahassee Democrat*. In addition to his sweet missive to me, he also wrote to the president of the Orlando Gator Club, suggesting all of their members who were businessmen withhold all advertising in the *Sentinel* until I was fired.

Several of those businessmen shook their heads sadly and sent me copies of the letter. Editors at the *Sentinel* shook their heads and laughed at the coach's pretentiousness. Also, to his dismay, they failed to fire me during my remaining seven years at the paper before voluntarily retiring in 2000.

Spurrier kept his word about not talking to me, although I often called to give him the opportunity to comment on any news story or column I felt he should be allowed to offer "his side." Well, he did actually speak to me once during that period. I was in Chicago on business and the founder of the Celebrity Golf Association invited me to play in the CGA tournament there, in which Spurrier was a contestant. I sidled up to his golf cart just to say hello and he was shocked to run into me so far from home.

"What are you doing up here?" he demanded.

I told him I was in Chicago to sign a publishing contract for my newest book. "It's a book all about you," I said with a straight face. That was mean of me. There was no such book in the works. He probably didn't sleep a wink that night.

SPURRIER'S absurd notion that sportswriters should be fawning "house men" for the teams they cover was overtly demonstrated in the 1994 season when he benched All-American wide receiver Jack Jackson for the first half of Florida's homecoming game against decidedly underdog Southern Mississippi. The suspension had not been announced and pulsing speculation coursed through the pressbox after the Gators had gone several offensive series while Jackson mysteriously remained on the bench in full uniform. Jackson played well in the second half, catching four passes for 78 yards in the easy victory and the media corps flocked to Jackson's locker when the dressing room doors were flung open for the press snoops. Jackson, however, had slipped out a back door to avoid being interviewed. An enterprising reporter, Chris Harry of the *Tampa Tribune*, had visited Jackson at his Moss Point, Mississippi home prior to the season for a profile story and had established a friendly relationship with the star. He also had Jackson's dorm phone number, which he dialed to seek comment about the mysterious half-game suspension.

From his room in the athletic dorm under the east stands of the stadium, Jackson said he had been a few minutes late for a practice that week when his small child became sick and had to be picked up from day care. No excuse, intoned the coach, who suspended him for the first half of the approaching Southern Miss game. Jackson made it clear he thought the suspension was unfair and Harry printed his comments.

Apparently, there was never an acceptable excuse for keeping the Ball Coach waiting. One of the top quarterback prospects in the country, Daunte Culpepper, lived a half-hour right down Interstate 75 in Ocala. He accepted an invitation to attend a Gators game and meet with Spurrier in his office a few hours before kickoff. A very elderly gentleman with an old clunker of a car in Daunte's low-end neighborhood volunteered to drive Culpepper to Gainesville for the meeting. Halfway there, a violent rainstorm forced the old gent to pull over on the side of the road to wait out the downpour. The pause made Daunte a few minutes late for his appointment.

Before Culpepper could explain his delay, Spurrier launched into a terse commentary about how everyone in the Gator football program is expected to be punctual and never, never, never make the Head Ball Coach have to wait. The conversation never got around to football subjects or recruiting or academics as Spurrier continued his harrangue. Culpepper, a polite, respectful 18-year-old at the time, said only an occasional "yes, sir," or "no, sir," all the time thinking how nice those University of Central Florida coaches had been to him. Culpepper signed that winter with UCF and went on to a spectacular college career and several seasons in the NFL.

Jackson's published comments taking issue with the Ball Coach was not the only bruise to Spurrier's considerable ego during that 1994 season.

Beat writer Robbie Andreau for the hometown *Gainesville Sun*, in a pregame assessment of an approaching crucial home game against undefeated Auburn, gave the coaching edge to Auburn's Terry Bowden, of all people. Robbie noted that he was just going along with Spurrier's midweek comment that Auburn's coaches must be doing a better job than him. Inflamed, Spurrier hot-footed to the *Sun's* editor, demanding that Robbie be taken off the Gator beat. Andreau, a UF alumnus and admitted avid Gator fan, was allowed to continue on the beat.

The Bowdens had become a nemesis for Spurrier. Florida State's Bobby Bowen had compiled a dominant head-to-head record against Spurrier. And now here was Bobby's son, Terry, pouring salt in the wounds. The Ball Coach took joy in denigrating Terry, who stands just 5-foot-6, by referring to him in public as Buster Brown ("who lived in a shoe").

But Terry stood tallest in this particular game in UF's daunting "Swamp," scoring a victory with multiple assists from a most unexpected source: Spurrier, himself. Several publications, including *Sports Illustrated*, noted that Spurrier had helped fire up Auburn's Tigers with demeaning comments during the week, threatening his own quarterback Terry Dean with a quick hook (his confidence shattered, Dean threw four interceptions before being yanked in favor of Danny Wuerffel), and letting his pass-happy bravado get the best of him when Florida could have run out the clock to preserve a narrow lead in the closing minutes. Auburn intercepted Wuerffel with 1:20 left, scored quickly for a 36-33 win and Spurrier was saddled with the bitter task of reaching DOWN to congratulate another Bowden.

It had been a bad week for the Ball Coach and he proceeded to make it worse with a strange, emotional outburst when the media gathered a few days later for their regular weekly meeting with Spurrier. After a brief Q&A, Spurrier excused the TV and radio reporters and honed in on the beat writers. He asked them to bring their tape recorders to the front and turn them off so he could make some personal observations.

He quickly became emotional, visibly fighting back tears as he said the Gators could have a great program if only the writers would get on board and stop the negative reporting. He berated Harry for making the call to Jack Jackson's dorm room and made the absurd accusation that Harry was "purposely looking for a negative story." Harry had long established himself as a fair and highly competent reporter. As the unusual sermon went on, the beat writers were nudging one another below the table and cutting their eyes side to side, perhaps charting a path to the nearest window or other escape route if the Ball Coach suddenly went postal.

One beat writer in the room that day assessed it as one of those "you're either with us or against us" talks. In Spurrier's universe, there is no such thing as an objective, even-handed reporter.

I've always thought of myself in that category and, indeed, I wrote many glowing columns about Spurrier's offensive skills and clean, disciplined program. We even played golf several times – once when he had just taken the Florida job. I had urged Florida in print to hire Spurrier, who was then having some success at lowly Duke, and I applauded the move when I broke the story that UF was about to hire him.

Weeks before that first season as UF coach, he called and expressed a desire to play golf with me at Arnold Palmer's Bay Hill Club, where I was a member. In the pro shop, Spurrier picked out a sweater vest with the Bay Hill logo, sneered at the price tag and asked a young clerk, "What's the price for the Florida ball coach?" The young man awkwardly explained that he didn't have authority to extend discounts.

"Well I don't want it then!" Spurrier snapped, tossing the sweater vest at the clerk and stalking off to the first tee.

I was left to apologize to the clerk, the club pro and Arnie for Florida's new "ball coach," who had just been awarded a multi-million dollar contract by UF.

ONE OF Spurrier's closest friends is former Cooper Tires sales executive Tom Kopplin. They met in a Gainesville bar a few days after Spurrier had been hired as head coach of the Tampa Bay Bandits of the short-lived United States Football League. Seated at the bar, Spurrier and Kopplin struck up a conversation with an attractive young lady, who wasn't aware she was seated next to one of the all-time football greats for the hometown Florida Gators.

Spurrier told her his name and she shrugged. Irritated, he pressed, emphasizing he once won the Heisman while playing for the Gators. "Oh, that's some kind of award, isn't it?" she said. When the woman departed, Spurrier and Kopplin began to talk. Both being single-handicap amateur golfers, Spurrier suggested they play sometime.

Kopplin offered to play Spurrier in a money golf match. Spurrier proposed that Kopplin show up at the Gainesville Country Club the next day and they would have a match. "Just remember, I'm not giving you any strokes," he said.

"Fine with me," said Kopplin.

When they were ready to tee off the next day, Spurrier emphasized again that he would not give Kopplin any strokes and proposed a $50 Nassau wager with 2-down automatic presses. "Fine with me," Kopplin repeated.

Kopplin won the match and several presses for a total of $400 and Spurrier squealed: "You hustled me!"

"No I didn't. I asked for no strokes and you made all the terms for the match," said Kopplin.

Eventually, Spurrier got over the loss and the two became close friends. Kopplin is the kind of friend the coach sorely needed. Unlike most of Spurrier's cronies, Kopplin has been a loyal friend without being a suck-up and speaks his mind if he feels the coach is out of line in any way. He remains as one of the very few who can converse with the Ball Coach objectively without being tossed overboard.

Spurrier's 12-year run as Florida's coach produced unprecedented results for the school's football program: (122-27-1 record, a national title, 6 Southeastern Conference titles, 11 bowl appearances). But along the way, he also constructed a dark record of disrespecting not only objective writers, but opposing coaches and fans. He disparaged Georgia Coach Ray Goff by publicly promising UF booster groups he would "never lose to Georgia as long as Ray 'Goof' is their coach." He ridiculed rival fans for complaining when he shamelessly ran up the score when any other coach would graciously run out the clock. Legendary college football commentator Keith Jackson said in a formal interview if he had been one of those coaches, "when I met Spurrier at midfield to shake hands after the game, I would have instead punched him in the nose."

Spurrier fired blistering shots at FSU's widely-admired Bobby Bowden, whom he claimed was teaching FSU teams to play dirty. The ethics committee of the American Football Coaches Association called him on the carpet for such remarks about another coach, but when he stood before the committee he said if they expected him to recant his comments they could forget it. He then promptly walked out of the meeting room.

Spurrier's stint at Florida ended with the 2001 season, which produced yet another controversy with the coach threatening legal action against Bowden and FSU. The Gators' star running back Earnest Graham suffered a knee ding in the game and Spurrier loudly claimed Graham had been intentionally injured under a pileup by FSU defensive star Darnell Dockett. A few days later, Spurrier advocated filing a law suit against Dockett, Bowden and the FSU football program – an unseemly move that many of even the most avid Gator boosters saw as embarrassing. Some of them urged the coach to drop the lawsuit talk and concentrate instead on the

Gators' approaching mismatch against underdog Maryland in the Orange Bowl. That only made him madder.

Spurrier and the Gators won the bowl game easily, but he had spent much of his time having his agent put out the word to NFL teams that he was ready to resign at Florida and consider one of the several feelers NFL teams had put out to him over the prior several years. "If the (UF) administration and boosters aren't going to back me in suing Florida State, then I'll just leave," he rationalized.

Shortly after the Orange Bowl, Spurrier signed a 5-year, $25 million contract to coach the NFL Washington Redskins. It was the largest contract ever for an NFL coach at that time. Meshing his over-wrought ego with that of equally overpaid and self-absorbed NFL players was a disaster. The Redskins were 12-20 in two years under Spurrier, who quit with three years left on his contract.

Florida was in the market for a new coach again and Spurrier allowed as how he would be willing to come back. But he had underestimated how Florida had grown weary of his antics. UF instead hired Urban Meyer and Spurrier eventually got back into college coaching at South Carolina.

THE TEARY rant to the beat writers a few days after that Jack Jackson half-game suspension was hardly the only time those in Spurrier's presence suspected he was not a rational, mentally rounded human being. The summer before quarterbacking icon Peyton Manning's final season at New Orleans' Newman High School, Peyton made a mini-tour of several colleges where he felt he might consider a scholarship offer the following winter. The idea was to view the facilities, talk with some players and, mainly, have a talk with the head coaches about their football philosophies. One stop on the tour was the office of Steve Spurrier.

Before Peyton had hardly settled into a chair across the desk from Spurrier, the coach went to great lengths to explain the trophy golf balls there in his office – each to commemorate Spurrier's various holes-in-one.

With that done, Spurrier then blurted: "I just want you to know that we really hate Georgia around here."

The conversation drifted to the coach's successful style of aggressive passing offense. But by then, Manning could have been excused if he had asked to see Spurrier's ink-blot tests. That night, he phoned home to his father, the legendary Archie Manning, to discuss the somewhat bizarre interview. The Mannings had been attracted to Spurrier's emphasis on passing and reputation for developing top quarterbacks. But now Florida was pretty much ruled out of the Peyton Derby. The young Manning eventually signed with Tennessee, where he played out his full four years of college eligibility before going on to become an NFL superstar.

(DURING THE first couple of years of my career, I regularly covered Archie at Ole Miss and during his first couple of NFL seasons with the woeful, expansion New Orleans Saints. So it was only fitting that more than two decades later, I closed my time as a newspaper columnist with occasional pieces on Peyton, whose unconditional love for his father came through loud and clear.)

He was a junior at Tennessee when I was given the opportunity to hold a lengthy, one-on-one interview with him two days before the important annual meeting of the Vols and Florida Gators. The interview was conducted in the lobby of the Vols' athletic dorm and my wife, Mary, happily tagged along. Both of us held the whole Manning family in high regard and Peyton knew I had covered Archie extensively.

Nevertheless, I reminded Peyton that I enjoyed interacting with Archie as a player, adding: "I guess you get tired of all of us old sports writer goats talking to you about him."

"Oh, no, sir," he replied firmly. "I'm very proud of my dad and I'll talk about him all you want."

That respectful remark put a giddy look on my wife's face that said she was trying hard not to jump over the couch to hug Peyton's neck.

There have been other times when Spurrier's demeanor in office meetings left others scratching their heads. Following Spurrier's senior season as a player at Florida, Miami Dolphins General Manager Joe Thomas was high on the Gators quarterback and went to Gainesville to talk to him in his agent's office. During the meeting, Spurrier picked up a deck of cards and began playing solitaire, hardly looking up as Thomas and the agent discussed the upcoming NFL draft. Spurrier barely engaged in the conversation.

Non-plussed, Thomas returned to Miami and decided to pick Bob Griese in the draft. Griese went on to a Hall of Fame career with the Dolphins. Spurrier was an NFL bust, sitting on the bench at San Francisco and then went winless as the starter for the expansion Tampa Bay Bucs.

But his legacy as a college coach includes a national title, those SEC crowns and lots of victories. And one thing more: quitter.

During his giddy run as Florida coach, there were several occasions when a game was going poorly that he threw down not only his trademark visor, but his head set and walked away when his quarterback came off the field. The body language said you guys are embarrassing me and I don't even want to talk to you. Late in a few games where a comeback was not impossible, Spurrier declined to call timeouts the Gators still had to stop the clock. The Ball Coach had quit.

When the UF administration and boosters failed to back his silly proposal to sue Bobby Bowden and FSU for allegedly teaching the Seminoles to intentionally harm his players, he quit and ran off to the NFL. After compiling a woeful 12-20 record as boss of the Washington Redskins, he quit, leaving three contract years on the table.

Shortly before the 2015 season at South Carolina, he called a press conference in which he bitterly used the word "enemies" 32 times in a 10-minute rant. He claimed he had no thoughts about retiring -- as some evil writers had suggested -- and claimed his current team was among the best he had had at South Carolina. Don't listen to those enemies, he said – i.e. sports writers and rival coaches. Halfway through the season, with his conference record at an embarrassing 0-4, he quit for good, leaving the program in the lurch.

Chapter 10 – Don Shula

On my airplane ride to Houston to cover the 1974 Super Bowl between the Miami Dolphins and Minnesota Vikings for the *Orlando Sentinel*, I happened to read a magazine story about how paranoid many college and pro coaches were about the despicable possibility of enemy spies watching their practice sessions. One of the coaches featured in the piece was legend-in-making Don Shula of the Dolphins.

In more recent years, New England Patriots Coach Bill Belichick became the leading NFL suspect for such nefarious activity. In fact, when the Patriots became embroiled with the "deflategate" scandal long after Shula retired, he openly referred to the Pats coach as "Bill Beli-cheat."

As my plane approached Houston Continental, I decided to pursue a story on how the two Super Bowl coaches dealt with the specter of practice spying. Once on the ground, a *Sentinel* colleague who outranked me suggested an angle: I should take our *Sentinel* photographer to the Dolphins' practice and photograph Shula's reaction as I exposed myself atop some nearby building as if spying on the Dolphins' "Super"-secret plays. Being young and foolish and ever on the prowl for some different story angle, I embraced the ill-conceived scenario.

Next day, photographer Frank Russell and I scouted out a three-story apartment building right across the street from the Dolphins' assigned practice field. We were hoping to find some resident willing for us to use their balcony for this tomfoolery, but instead found an easy access to the roof. At the height of Miami's practice, I unfolded to my full 5-foot-7 atop the building, wearing a properly sinister overcoat (with the collar turned up, of course, for effect) and peering through binoculars. Russell snapped photos of me and of players, coaches and – gulp! – *security officers* as they went into full five-alarm alert at the sight of the rooftop "spy."

Equipment manager Charlie Wade dashed to where Shula was standing and directed his attention to the building roof. Shula visibly gasped and began barking battlefield commands. The security guys scrambled toward the apartment building as Russell and I scrambled to our rental car. I am happy to report there were no arrests and no bullets fired as we made our escape.

The story and photographs ran in the *Sentinel* the next morning, Friday, January 11, 1974. Fridays of Super Bowl weeks feature the annual state-of-the-NFL address by the commissioner and the final pre-game press conferences for the two competing coaches. By then, I was having second thoughts about the journalistic propriety of posing as a practice spy. So at the end of Shula's press conference, I managed to intercept him as he was leaving the room. I wanted to assure him that the "spy" at his press conference the day before was neither an agent of the Vikings nor a KGB agent, but rather a misguided sports writer. Namely, me.

The look he gave me could have burned a hole through the door of a bank safe. "Why did you want to do that?!" he demanded. I meekly explained the story angle, apologized and said I should have declined my boss' suggestion. Shula stomped off shaking his head.

To his credit, the famed coach didn't have me arrested, scourged, or boiled in oil. In fact, he was always civil and accessible for me throughout the next two decades as I occasionally covered the Dolphins. He is one of those rare high-profile sports personalities able to bark at any annoying indiscretion, then get over it. Longtime Dolphins PR director Harvey Greene concurs. "If something goes wrong, dealing with Coach was like dealing with an approaching thunderstorm. The jaw would set and you might get hit with a bolt or two. But then it was over. He would usually say something soon afterward to put you at ease."

DON SHULA was always suspicious of strange faces that showed up not just on rooftops, but also in his locker room.

A year after the Dolphins' 1972 perfect season, noted author James Michener turned up for a Dolphins game against the New York Jets in Shea Stadium, as guest of Dolphins owner Joe Robbie. Michener was putting together a book called "Sports in America" which was published in 1974. After the game, Robbie escorted the famed author to the interview room so he could get a feel for what goes on when Shula addresses the media in his post-game press conferences.

Almost immediately after entering the room, Shula spotted Michener with a notepad and noticed there was no proper credential hanging around his neck. He asked an aide who the guy was. "A writer," said the aide. "A writer?!!" Shula snorted. "Get him outta here!"

So the great James Michener was unceremoniously tossed from Shula's post-game press conference. I guess the sage coach knew none of the rest of us were actual writers.

AFTER A GAME in Miami, another unfamiliar face showed up, wearing a cap emblazoned with "Miami Vice" on the crown. The reference was to the television show which, at the time, was at its height of popularity. The guy in the cap was the star of the series, who was allowed in the locker room and introduced to Shula as, simply, Don Johnson. Shula noticed the wording on his cap and shook hands with the stranger.

"Coach Shula, it's an honor to meet you," said Johnson. "I want to salute you for your success and thank you for all you do for this community."

"No, no," the coach protested. "Thank YOU for all _you_ do for this community. You guys do a great job fighting crime."

Johnson blinked awkwardly and suggested that the coach might want to attend a shoot. "A shoot?!," the coach exclaimed. "Wouldn't that be dangerous?" Then someone explained to Shula that Johnson was a television actor, not a vice cop.

Obviously, the super-focused football coach spent his evenings watching game films, not shoot 'em up TV detective shows.

ON HIS DAY off one week during the season, Dolphins defensive tackle Manny Fernandez took a junket into the Everglades with a guide and managed to capture a live small alligator of about four feet in length. He brought it back to the Dolphins' practice facility the next day and, after a discussion with several teammates about what to do with the agitated gator, decided to put it in Shula's private shower just off his office.

After practice, it was all the players could to do to keep a straight face when the coach walked through the locker room en route to his office. A minute later, Shula shot out into the main locker room like a frightened gazelle. Perhaps wearing a towel. Perhaps not. His face contorted with pure anger as he focused on fun-loving running back Jim Kiick, who was renowned for his practical jokes.

"Why are you coming after me?" Kiick said, innocently, fending off the coach. "You ought to be thanking me. We took a vote and I was the deciding vote to tape the gator's mouth shut."

SHULA WAS NEVER much for tearing himself away from football to take a vacation, but first wife Dorothy managed to drag him out of town for a short vacation after one of the Dolphins' Super Bowl appearances. They took a brief getaway to a quiet village in Maine and decided one evening to go to a movie. When they walked into the small theater, the few people there, to Shula's surprise, began applauding.

Flattered, the coach smiled and waved and told one of the movie goers, "I didn't think anyone would recognize me all the way up here."

Said the guy: "I don't really know who you are, but the projector operator said he wouldn't start the movie until there were at least 12 people here. You and your wife make 12, so we can now see the movie."

(Note: Former Florida State coach Bobby Bowden heard this Shula anecdote and liked it so much he commandeered it for some of his banquet talks. Except he inserted his and his wife's names in place of the Shulas and occasionally told the story as if it had happened to him. Shame on you, Bobby.)

KEEPING A TIME SCHEDULE was always imperative for Shula. Sometime during the '80s, the Dolphins flew into Providence, RI, for a game against the New England Patriots. As usual, the schedule called for the team to bus directly to the Pats' stadium in Foxboro for a light workout.

The window of opportunity to conduct the workout was limited because the stadium crew was trying to prepare the field for the game the next day. When the Dolphins' charter came to a halt on the tarmac, the stairs were wheeled out to the plane and attendants began pumping up the stairs to reach the plane's door. During the process, the pump failed and the stairs were still well below the open door.

Standing in the plane's open doorway, Don Shula tried to grasp the problem.

On the ground, the Dolphins official who was advancing the game frantically called the airport director and asked for another set of stairs to be moved into place. The word was that the only other set of stairs were at the far end of the terminal and it would take 20 minutes or so to get them moved to the Dolphins' charter. The club official tried to shout an update to the impatient coach, who was still standing in the doorway and obviously agitated that his practice time was ticking way. But airport noise drowned out his shouts.

Finally, the backup stairs arrived and Shula and the Dolphins were allowed to disembark. Shula was noticeably irritated and wondered aloud if the delay was going to prevent the team workout. As he passed the team advance man, he scowled and said, "Add this to your bleeping checklist."

NEAR THE END of his storied, 26-year run as Miami coach, whispers began to circulate that Shula's demeanor was softening and that was part of the reason the Dolphins had become much less dominant in the AFC East. The Dolphins were an un-Shula-like 9-7 in two of his final three seasons and won the AFC East division title only twice in his final ten seasons.

Those around the coach, who had been such a driven, no-nonsense taskmaster most of his coaching career, began to see some softening around the edges. It may have been because he was in love.

Longtime wife Dorothy Shula died of breast cancer in February, 1991. More than a year later, he began a courtship with his second wife, wealthy socialite Mary Anne Stephens. It was noticed that Shula dressed more fashionably, laughed more easily and began to take interest in the world outside football. Toward the end of the 1992 season, Mary Anne was part of the travel party to Dolphin road games.

For years, the routine for road games called for a Dolphins staffer to spend several days prior to games in the opposing city, building a file of local clippings on the hometown team. Shula's aim was to pore over the stories in search of minor injuries or any other bits of information that might hint at a weakness in the other team. When the Dolphins arrived at the end of the week, the staffer's task was to meet the plane and immediately deliver the clippings file to Shula as he disembarked. It was always the first thing the coach asked for and he'd begin eagerly reading the clips en route to the team hotel.

On this one occasion, however, when the staffer handed the file to Shula, he poked it into his brief case and asked instead if the staffer had followed his instructions to have a spray of flowers delivered to Mary

Anne's room. I wrote about that departure of routine as an indication of Shula's evolving demeanor.

On the next road trip, I called his room and requested a short interview on the eve of that game. For the first time since the "spy" caper years earlier, Shula barked at me for writing the flowers anecdote. Then he invited me to his room for the requested chat. Bless you, Don Shula.

Chapter 11 – Walt Zembriski

New Jersey urchin Walt Zembriski was never a golf icon, but he became, undoubtedly, the quintessential Walter Mitty saga. Between dangerous stints as a steelworker atop rising skyscrapers just across the Hudson River from Manhattan, Walt became an accomplished, self-taught amateur golfer at Mahwah's Out of Bounds Golf Club, where his father had frequently caddied for baseball's legendary Babe Ruth. Walt first gained attention as a golfer when the scruffy little man won the Metropolitan Golf Association's prestigious Eisenhower Amateur in 1964, defeating dozens of country-club-honed amateurs in stylish doubleknits.

He celebrated the next day by going right back up atop the steel skeleton of another rising building, an occupation that came with the sobering memories of watching, over time, four co-workers plunge to their deaths. Walt nearly became No. 5 one windswept afternoon when he was bending steel rods at the corner of a rising building that had reached 10 stories.

A crane operator lifted a load of lumber framing and swung it across the top. High winds took over, pushing the load too far across the top of the building. Walt was trapped on the opposite corner of that floor as the head-high stack of lumber came skimming across the top floor directly at him. With nowhere to turn, he leaped onto the side of the stack and held on as it continued out into thin air.

A foreman on the ground on that side of the building, shocked by the sight of Walt's legs dangling from the stack, frantically radioed the crane operator, instructing him to quickly lower the wood stack to the ground as Walt gripped tighter and tighter. "When I reached the ground," Zembriski recalls, "you could see my *fingerprints* in that wood!"

He then had the decision all high steelworkers face after a near-fatal accident. "If you don't go right back up, you lose your nerve and can never let yourself go up there again. But I needed the work. So I went down the street to a bar and, after a couple of stiff drinks, went right back up on that building."

A couple years later, Walt tried another occupation where sweating over four-foot putts seemed certainly less stressful and far more rewarding than $13-an-hour hammering red-hot steel rivets 300 feet above the Hudson. Staked by his father-in-law, who owned a small construction company, Walt turned pro and briefly took a crack at the PGA Tour. He managed to start 10 events, but won just $3,088, not enough to cover expenses. Dispirited and broke, he returned to Mahwah and fetched his construction helmet out of the closet. Weekends was back to Out-of-Bounds, where he could hustle golf bets. The father-in-law and the wife gave up on Walt, who appeared to have no future.

He had read a magazine piece about the J.C. Goosie Mini-Tour in Central Florida, an enterprise where aspiring young golf pros could test their game and play for a modes purse funded by their own entry fees. In his mid-40s at the time, Walt drove his rusting Buick with nearly 200,000 miles on it to Orlando to chase his dream. He handed over $500 to Goosie, a former journeyman PGA Tour pro, for a series of three tournaments against hot shot flat-bellies half his age. Walt won 15 Goosie events over the next five years, but the payoffs were limited and he had to work small jobs on the side to keep a flop-house roof over his head. During a slump or two, he actually slept in the old Buick alongside assorted practice balls, old clubs, balls, empty Coke cans and other refuse. Goosie, who admired Walt's dawn-to-dusk practice regimen, loaned him entry money on occasion.

One of the part-time jobs Walt took on was handyman at public Cypress Creek Golf Course just for the privilege of practicing and playing there between stints as the club painter, pool cleaner, etc. That was the preamble for one of the greatest golf-hustling episodes since gutta met percha.

A slacker named Rick Robineau owned the club, which his wealthy mother had bought for him hoping Rick would finally make something of himself. One day he was playing cards with a couple of Tennessee hustlers in the locker room while our little hero, 5-7, 150-pound Walter Joseph Zembriski, was atop a step ladder painting the room. Robineau won a couple hundred dollars in the card game and the visitors proposed a golf match, to give them a shot at winning back their money.

"Hell, I'll take my painter up there and whip you guys," challenged Robineau, motioning up toward the unlikely handyman. The Tennessee pair took one look at Walt's paint-specked T-shirt, faded jeans and shaggy hair and virtually ran to the first tee. Robineau instructed Walt to take a break and get ready for a big-money golf match and promised to cover Walt's side of the bets. Walt said he needed time to change clothes, but Robineau insisted Walt play just as he was unimpressively dressed.

The painter shot 67. The Tennessee hustlers departed, $800 lighter.

MONITORING THE budding PGA Senior Tour on TV and in the *Orlando Sentinel*, Walt noticed he was posting better scores on tougher courses than the Senior Tour pros were playing at that time. If only he could hold out until he turned 50 -- minimum age for the new Senior Tour – Walt was confident he could beat those famous old guys if only given the chance.

Walter Mitty fully emerged in 1985 when Zembriski turned 50 and survived qualifying rounds to earn a spot in the USGA Senior Open at Lake Tahoe – a major event on the new Senior Tour. After a friend loaned him air fare, he showed up in Tahoe with just $260 to his name. Shocking the big-name stars, Walt led the tournament for two-and-half rounds. He was just two strokes off the lead going into the final round, but was dead tired. He had been too nervous to sleep and wound up repeatedly walking up and down five floors of stairs in his hotel in an attempt to tire himself into slumber.

Miller Barber, the storied "Mr. X" of tour fame, surged to win and Walt held on for a fourth-place finish worth a soothing $9,000 payoff. He didn't have enough cash left to pay his caddie. Walt assumed it would be like the Goosie Mini-Tour, where the winners hung around the bar following the final round until J.C. doled out the cash. This time, however, a USGA official asked for Walt's bank routing numbers where his $9000 could be wired.

Walt was too proud to admit he didn't HAVE a bank account and said he would have to call in the routing numbers after he returned to Orlando. A friend loaned him enough money to pay the caddie and open the bank account when he returned home.

But that was only the first hurdle in reaching his pro golf fantasy. The Senior Tour at that time was a closed shop. Even after the high finish in the Senior Open, Walt would be required to play his way into each Senior Tour event the rest of that year in long-odds Monday qualifiers. There were usually more than 80 qualifiers shooting for just four to six spots in the tournament that week. Remarkably, Zembriski was 4-for-5 in that summer's qualifiers, but still had to endure sneers and gamesmanship from Dan Sikes, Bob Goalby and other Senior Tour regulars who didn't embrace the idea of a former steelworker horning in on their second-career windfall.

At a Lexington, Ky., tournament sponsored in part by a Marriott hotel, Walt won a qualifying spot and excitedly raced over to the Marriott, where he heard the tournament competitors were being given free rooms that week. He had never stayed at a Marriott and could only imagine the luxuries. After some awkward moments at the front desk, the hotel's manager came out and informed Walt that the comp rooms were only for the regular Senior Tour players, not for qualifiers.

Walt retreated, his gut churning, back across the street to his $27 room at the Knight's Inn.

After 54 regulation holes, four players were tied — Lee Elder, Orville Moody, Sikes and guess who. Elder won on the third playoff hole, but the other three were also invited to a post-tournament reception at that Marriott. That same manager who had haughtily rebuffed him earlier in the week, sidled up to Walt and assured him he would be welcome at the Marriott the next year.

"Not me, pal," Walt sniffed pridefully. "I kinda like it over at the Knight's Inn."

Another challenge Walt The Interloper often faced was simply accessing the players' locker room. The regulars were issued handsome money clips that identified them as full-fledged members of the Senior Tour. Qualifiers were given paper credentials to be tied onto a belt loop. At Charlotte, Walt was stopped at the locker room door by a security guard, who had taken one look at Walt's shaggy hair, rumpled white golf shirt and red pants with the two cigarette holes and assumed he must have pilfered the credential. The guard snatched it away and advised Walt the caddie pen was around back. A PGA tournament official had to come to the rescue. Being mistaken for some worker bee was nothing new for Walt. Years earlier, he had qualified to play in the U.S. Open at Cherry Hill in Denver. Player locker assignments were alphabetical and Walt was lockered next to Tour star Tom Weiskopf. Following the second round, Weiskopf unlaced his golf shoes and extended them toward Walt, adding: "Clean these and open my locker, please."

"I'd be happy to," Walt retorted, "but I'm not a locker boy. I'm playing in the tournament. In fact, if you check the scoreboard, you'll find that I'm one shot ahead of you!"

If Zembriski in an opulent locker room seems like a frog in silk pajamas to Weiskopf, well, Walt would agree. "They give you a locker at every tournament, but I didn't often use them. I just wasn't comfortable in there. Those other guys like (Sam) Snead and (Julius) Boros sat around and reminisced, but I didn't have anything to reminisce with them about."

Following that first year as a weekly qualifier on the Senior Tour, Walt defied long odds again by winning one of just four 1986 spots available at the annual Senior Tour Q-School to earn his full membership for the '87 season. There were 92 competitors and Walt finished second. Quickly he developed a huge following of gas station attendants, postmen, factory workers and others accustomed to dragging pull-carts over dusty public courses. Golf manufacturers showered him with new clubs, shoes, balls and golf gloves, hoping to get his signature on endorsement contracts.

Back home in his tiny apartment, Walt proudly showed me a box of a dozen new gloves one company had sent. "Until this, I wasn't getting nothin'," he grinned. "I couldn't even get a golf ball. I can't remember when I had more than one new glove." Sometimes, it was a soiled and worn glove he plucked out of a trash bin that he judged had a few rounds left in it.

Having ascended to become a full-fledged Senior Tour regular, Walt flourished, proving he was right that he could beat these famed old guys. He won three tournaments including the 1988 Vantage Championship in North Carolina where first-place money was $130,000 – largest on the Senior Tour to that date. He hurried off to the airport to fly home, unaware there was a toney coat-and-tie champion's dinner that night. Tournament officials intercepted Walt in the airport, but he had already checked his luggage . So he attended as the guest of honor wearing the frayed golf shirt and red slacks (with the two cigarette burn holes) that he had worn during the final round that day.

THE MONEY kept pouring in and Walt bought a red Cadillac with a "Z-Man" license plate and a small condo at the golf course where he once was the painter/pool cleaner. That bank kept calling to warn his account had overflowed again. His checking account was guaranteed only up to $100,000, so each time those wired Tour payoffs ran over, he bought a $50,000 certificate of deposit. Some five years into his Senior Tour career, I noticed a thick stack of what appeared to be financial instruments on his kitchen counter, bound by a rubber band. Walt explained those were his CDs and laughed gleefully as he riffled them like a deck of cards. We counted. They totaled $1.2 million.

Out on the Tour, fellow players like Bobby Nichols urged Walt to invest in stocks, noting that CDs paid "only" about six percent interest at the time. Plenty for Walt, who was not far removed from sleeping in the Buick and liked the safety of CDs. Then the dot-com bust hit the market and Walt would playfully chortle at Nichols and the others, asking them, "How are your *Ciscos* doing now? What about your *AOLs*?" Yuk, yuk, yuk.

WALT WOULD LEARN there were other pitfalls for his new-found wealth. One was a women who moved in with him and kept pushing him to get married. She even had business cards printed that said, "Cheryl Zembriski," but Walt resisted. To appease her, he hired her to handle his travel arrangements and pay bills. When he took time to look closer, he discovered she had bilked him for more than six figures and he kicked her out.

At the season-ending Senior Tour Championship in Puerto Rico, Walt lamented to anyone who would listen that he had been scammed by his live-in girlfriend. He told the story to one player too many: outspoken Dave Hill. Over breakfast, Hill listened to the tale of woe, then asked a question. "How many times did you have sex with this woman?"

Walt shrugged and replied: "I dunno. Maybe a hundred?"

"Well, Walt, my man," said Hill. "That's just the screwing you get for the screwing you got!"

Everyone at the table laughed. Including the quintessential Walter Mitty of golf.

Chapter 12 – Mike Shanahan, Charley Pell

MIKE SHANAHAN is just one of many prominent football coaches with northern or western backgrounds who discovered that southern college football would be something of a culture shock. After one season as an assistant coach at the University of Minnesota, the young, Illinois-born Shanahan accepted the job of offensive coordinator at Florida under drawling, troubled head coach Charley Pell, who had just suffered an 0-10-1 first season in charge of the Gators. Pell grew up in rural Sand Hill, Alabama, and played for the Crimson Tide under Bear Bryant as an undersized, gritty lineman.

"It didn't take long to figure out how important football was in that part of the world. High school football, college football was a way of life down in Florida, Alabama, Georgia," recalls Shanahan. "In the Southeastern Conference, you learn very quickly that this is the most important thing going on. You also learned that it was the most talented conference, in my opinion. You start taking a look at players and how they were being drafted, you begin to appreciate what the SEC is all about."

With Shanahan installing a pro-type spread offense, the Gators rebounded to an 8-4 season, the largest, one-season turnaround in NCAA history. But working under Pell was an eye-opening experience. Mike made an effort to recruit Ohio schoolboy star quarterback Bernie Kosar.

During his four years at Florida, Shanahan spent a lot of time in Charley's house in the off-seasons, talking football strategy and recruiting. In the process, he discovered what a passionate Southerner his boss was. Kosar had many top programs after his signature, but Shanahan sensed he had established a good rapport with the blue-chip prospect. During one of those visits in Pell's home, Shanahan told the head coach, "I feel good about Bernie. I think Bernie's gonna come with us. I think we've got him."

Pell's response: "Aw, Mike, we've got too many Yankees around here already."

Shanahan was jolted by the unexpected comment. But he had to laugh nervously at Pell's next words: "Mike, you're the only Yankee I've ever liked."

Kosar went on to become a standout quarterback at the University of Miami and in the NFL.

SHANAHAN WOULD LEARN that Pell's dislike for Yankees was topped only by his disdain for NCAA investigators. The Gators fell under the scrutiny of the NCAA and eventually would be handed a severe probation that cost Pell his job. There was a telling meeting with one of the investigators, during which Shanahan came to realize the hammer would be falling. Shanahan sat next to the defiant Pell as the coaching staff was grilled by the investigator.

At one point, the NCAA official, seated directly across a conference table from Pell, slid a blank sheet of paper across and asked him to make a list of recruiting red flags. Pell wadded the sheet into a little ball and tossed it back across the table, hitting the official in the forehead. " That's when I knew Florida was going on probation," Mike recalled.

By the time the Gators were thrown in the NCAA jailhouse, Shanahan, who was not cited in any of the UF infractions, had moved up to the NFL as offensive coordinator for the Denver Broncos. After an ill-fated stint as head coach of the Raiders, he returned to Denver as quarterback coach and developed a tight relationship with young star quarterback John Elway. That caused some uneasiness on the part of Broncos head coach Dan Reeves. Shanahan was fired, but bounced right back as offensive coordinator for the high-flying San Francisco 49ers in 1992 and helped to lead the team to a magnificent 14-2 record. At the end of the season, Reeves was fired at Denver and Broncos owner Pat Bowlen offered the job to Shanahan. That set up a bizarre circumstance in which an NFL quarterback tried to personally hire his head coach.

In talks with Bowlen about the position, Shanahan was offered $400,000 and two cars, but Mike also insisted on having control of the full roster salary cap so he could manage the team personnel to assure the Broncos would be competitive. "If I took the head job at Denver, I wanted to have the full salary cap to work with and have a personal salary that would put me in the upper half of the NFL head coaches at that time," Shanahan would explain years later. "The salary was not that important as long as I felt we could be competitive. Bowlen resisted the salary cap stipulation, saying he didn't feel he could put that provision in writing."

So Shanahan declined the offer. Elway heard there were talks going on between Bowlen and Shanahan and excitedly called Mike to check the progress. Shanahan explained that he had decided to stay in San Francisco as coordinator. Distraught, Elway wanted to know why.

Shanahan told Elway about the money and the cars, but didn't feel he could discuss the salary cap request. He felt Elway might misunderstand his intention. All he would say was that the offer just wasn't right for him. Elway pressed, asking why he wasn't coming back to Denver and what it would take for the offer to be "right." Shanahan said he would need a salary of $500,000 and two cars, but didn't mention the salary cap provision.

"Well, I'll take care of the half-million and the two cars," said Elway. "So the money is solved and the cars are solved. So you're coming."

"No, John. I can't have you do that," said Shanahan. "That's the owner's responsibility. That's not your responsibility."

Shanahan stayed at San Francisco for two more seasons as offensive coordinator. The Denver head coach position opened again and this time Bowlen agreed to all of the terms set out by Shanahan, who would coach the Broncos for the next 13 seasons, including back-to-back Super Bowl titles in 1998 and 1999 with Elway under center.

So Elway got his favorite coach after all, and didn't have to pay him out of his own pocket.

"That offer by John just shows how competitive he is," Shanahan recounts. "He didn't care about the money. He just wanted to make sure the situation was such that we had the best chance to win. I confided with him about a year later that I had turned down Pat's first offer because of the salary cap issue. It was more than the just the money with me, too."

MUCH EARLIER in his career while an assistant coach at Florida, Shanahan developed a lasting friendship with athletic department official Jeremy Foley, who later would become athletic director after Mike left for a coaching job in the NFL. Foley would later make two unsuccessful attempts to lure Shanahan back to Florida as head coach. The first came when Steve Spurrier resigned to accept a huge contract as head coach of the NFL Washington Redskins. But Shanahan already had two Super Bowl titles under his belt as head coach of the Denver Broncos and was not interested in returning to the collegiate level.

The second came in 2014 – after Shanahan became Spurrier's successor at Washington and was fired after four seasons there. Will Muschamp was the Gators' coach at the time, struggling through a couple of mediocre seasons. In the summer of 2014, during preseason drills, Foley asked Shanahan to make a 3-day visit to Florida to evaluate UF's players and observe practices. Shanahan reluctantly granted the request from his old friend, though felt awkward about it.

The 2014 Gators season developed into another bummer, featuring weekly speculation about Muschamp's tenure. In late season, Muschamp was fired and Foley extended a secret feeler to his old pal to see if Shanahan would consider coaching in college again.

Shanahan told Foley he was interested only in pro football because he had been in the NFL so long, having been the head coach of the Raiders, Broncos and Redskins following a stellar stint as offensive coordinator during the San Francisco 49ers' dominance in the early '90s. "I didn't feel comfortable that people might think I was down there at the summer practices as a candidate. It just wasn't the right timing. When my name got thrown around, I was embarrassed that people would think I only went down there in the summer to take over Muschamp's job. I just didn't like the image," recounted the high-principled Shanahan.

ONE THING THAT Shanahan learned during his stint as Florida's coordinator was how shrewd Alabama icon Bear Bryant was. Then an impressionable young assistant coach, Shanahan was pleasantly surprised when he received an invitation to play in an early-summer golf tournament Bryant hosted in Tuscaloosa for a number of SEC assistant football coaches. Shanahan had not met Bryant at that point and eagerly accepted the invitation.

"I could tell that after a couple of cocktails, Coach Bryant was a lot of fun," Shanahan recalls. "He went out of his way to meet a lot of the coaches there. It kinda blew me away as a young coach that he would be that accessible."

Shanahan took note that Bryant was the only head coach at the event, but there were lots of assistant coaches and coordinators from all across the Southeastern Conference. They all talked football between the golf rounds as the Bear picked their brains.

"And the head coaches were letting that happen," Shanahan recalled incredulously. "I was really impressed with how ahead of the curve he was."

SHANAHAN'S FIRST stint as an NFL head coach was an eye-opening disappointment. Following impressive work as a college and NFL offensive coordinator, Mike got his shot as head coach of controversial Al Davis' then-Los Angeles Raiders. He was the first head coach from outside the Raiders organization and quickly learned that Al was in control of everything.

"Al would be out on the practice field and actually made substitutions if he thought a player had had enough. He didn't do it all the time, but I never had that happen to me before. He did it enough that I would say to myself, 'Holy cow! What have I gotten myself into?' "

 Shanahan would fire what he considered sub-par assistant coaches and Davis would hire them back. The divide grew wider as the season went on. Late in that season, the Raiders were playing Seattle at home with the AFC West title on the line. "We lost, but that shows that at least we were competitive," says Shanahan. "We started out the next year 1-3, followed by a bye week and, thus, had two weeks to prepare for the next game. That's when I was fired. In the prior 10 years, the Raiders had seven different head coaches. I lasted one season plus four games, so I called up some of those prior coaches and congratulated them for lasting longer than I did."

Needless to say, Shanahan was no longer an Al Davis admirer, but he had lots of company. Players, coaches and league officials throughout the NFL despised Davis. The next season, when Shanahan was offensive coordinator at San Francisco, he would face Davis again in a Monday Night game between the 49ers and the Raiders.

During warmups, Al Davis began wandering around on the Niners' end of the field, decked out in his gleaming white Elvis Presley jumpsuit, as San Francisco ran some plays. "Everyone on our team was unhappy that Al was out there on our end of the field watching our plays. So we ran a pass play with a receiver running right to where Al was standing. Some people thought Elvis Grbac threw the pass, but it was Steve Young. The ball came like a bullet right at Davis' head. I thought, 'Ohmigod! We just wanted to scare him. I didn't want to kill him.' "

At the last moment, Davis dove to the turf and came up spitting grass. His flamboyant white outfit was covered in dirt. A strong wind was blowing his hair everywhere. He glared at the 49ers and his long hair was all over his face. You couldn't even see his face.

"Our guys go crazy, they're laughing so hard," Shanahan recounts. "But after that game, Al Davis was never on the field again during our pregame warmups. He would stay well back of the sidelines."

IN THE GAME THAT NIGHT, star wideout Jerry Rice had a chance to pass the Raiders' Tim Brown as the NFL's all-time touchdown receiver. Jerry needed two to tie Brown and three to become No. 1. The Niners were comfortably ahead in the fourth quarter and Rice already had two touchdown catches. He needed just one more, but Rice and many of the other regulars were on the bench when the Niners took the field for their final possession, basically just to run out the clock.

Shanahan, calling plays from the pressbox, suggested to head coach George Seifert they allow Rice to go for the record. "Yeah, okay. Let's give it one shot," said Seifert. Back on the field came Young and Rice for one play. They ran up the score on Davis and the Raiders as Rice hauled in his third TD catch to claim the record. Rice would finish his career with a still-record 197 touchdowns, far ahead of Brown, the former Raider star. Take that, Al.

Chapter 13 – Davey Johnson

IN HIS FINAL season as the winningest manager in New York Mets history, Davey Johnson had had all he could take from tempestuous star slugger Darryl Strawberry's disruptive behavior. Strawberry was often late for team workouts, or missed them completely. He publicly complained about Johnson taking him out late in a game on a double-switch. He got into a physical altercation on team picture day with team captain Keith Hernandez and publicly threatened to punch out infielder Wally Bachman.

Davey kept fining Strawberry for his transgressions, but nothing seemed to work. Finally, in the visitors' clubhouse at Chicago's Wrigley Field, Johnson's patience boiled over and the then-47-year-old manager challenged the 28-year-old, 6-foot-6 problem child to fisticuffs. Johnson confronted Strawberry, his fists clenched like a prize fighter, his face contorted in anger.

"C'mon! C'mon! I've had all your shit I can take. Let's settle this once and for all!" Johnson shouted, his clenched fists churning.

Surprised and embarrassed, Strawberry remained seated on a stool in front of his locker as several teammates fell back into their lockers, hiding their laughter behind towels. Finally, Strawberry just hung his head and remained on the stool while Johnson chided the misbehaving star and eventually retreated to the manager's office. That proved to be a turning point in their relationship. Strawberry immediately began showing the respect for Johnson that had been missing.

I bumped into Strawberry in Orlando shortly after that season and mentioned that I was a friend and sometimes golfing companion of

Davey's. Strawberry launched into an unabashed profession of praise for Johnson.

Years later, Johnson looked back to that unsavory, but pivotal moment and had this to say: "I had become a father figure to Darryl, who grew up without a father. He had become a constant problem. He'd show up late and I would fine him $500 – but with the money always going to charity in an effort to turn a bad situation into something positive. It was like telling a son, 'I love you, but I can't let you do these things.'"

After his playing career ended and several brushes with the law that landed him in and out of jail, Strawberry pronounced himself a born-again Christian. He and current wife Tracy, whom he met at a drug recovery convention, established the successful Darryl Strawberry Foundation near St. Louis, dedicated to children with autism. Without the help of fine money. More recently, the couple moved to Orlando and he gives talks to youths about the pitfalls of drug use.

A footnote – Only five players in MLB history have hit two pinch-hit, grand slam homers in the same season. Two of those players are Davey Johnson and Darryl Strawberry.

IN THE SPRING of 1975, Davey Johnson was an established star for the Atlanta Braves, having hit 43 homeruns two seasons earlier – an all-time record for second basemen. The Braves played the Tokyo Giants of the Japan League in a spring exhibition and the visitors were sufficiently impressed with Johnson to express a desire for him to sign with the team and return to Japan with them.

The Braves were being difficult in negotiating a new contract with Davey, who welcomed the overtures from the Tokyo club. The working agreement between Major League Baseball and the Japan League called for the acquiring club to pay a fee to the player's current club just for the rights to attempt signing him. The Braves proposed that the Giants pay the Braves $160,000 to talk to Johnson.

"The Braves thought I was an idiot," Davey recalls. Instead, he pulled a shrewd move: He convinced the Braves he would not re-sign with them, so they placed him on waivers, hoping to collect a waiver fee from any club that claimed him. But he let everyone in baseball management know he intended to sign with Tokyo, so he cleared waivers and became a free agent. Once that was accomplished, Davey told the Tokyo Giants if they would pay him – not the Braves -- the $160,000 as a signing bonus he would play for them under whatever they agreed would be a "fair" one-year contract.

During the waiver process, Johnson received a phone call from college coaching icon Bear Bryant. The two knew one another because many years earlier Bryant had been the football coach at Texas A&M when Johnson was playing baseball there. The Bear tried to talk Davey out of going to Japan, reasoning, "You're an American and you don't need to go play in some foreign country. Your legacy should be as an American ballplayer."

Why would Bear Bryant be motivated to advise Johnson? Simple. He had become friends with controversial Charlie Finley, then owner of the Kansas City Athletics and Finley thought the Bear might have some sway with Johnson. It didn't work. Johnson politely told the legendary football coach he was going to keep his options open. It turns out that Finley had plans to pick up the waiver on Johnson, but withdrew it after the report back from Bryant.

So Johnson signed a $100,000 contract with the Giants, plus the $160K signing bonus. As a token for their fumble, Davey voluntarily gave the Braves a $10,000 stipend out of that signing bonus. Bottom line: The Braves wound up with ten grand, a hole in their infield and a lot of egg on the face of then-general manager Eddie Robinson. And Davey Johnson, a quarter-million dollars richer, was off to the Japan League for a new adventure in his never-dull baseball career as a player and manager.

THINGS DIDN'T GO as well as Davey had hoped during the outset of his time in Japan. At the time, I was a columnist for the *Orlando Sentinel* and Johnson, who grew up in the Orlando suburb, Winter Park, was considered local news. About a month into Davey's time as a Tokyo Giant, I managed to arrange a trans-Pacific phone interview that was memorable. Johnson was painfully homesick and became emotional. Clear sobbing could be heard as he ticked off the problems he faced.

His team-assigned interpreter didn't speak much English. Japanese food staples consisted of slippery entrees that seemed to be trying to slide off his plate and back to sea. He was hit in the back by a pitch, hard enough to break a bone, in one of those early games and it took him weeks to regain his effective batting stroke. Plus, in Japanese baseball culture the theory is if you start a game badly, you'll also finish badly. Being a power hitter, it was normal for Johnson to often strike out in that first at-bat. When it happened, his manager, beloved Japan League hall of famer Shigeo Nagashima, pulled him for a pinch-hitter next time up. Since he couldn't understand what anyone was saying – including his interpreter – Davey was at a loss to absorb the operative theory and was embarrassed at being lifted for a pinch-hitter.

He also developed some sort of infection in his thumb that refused to heal. The club referred him to a Japanese doctor who wanted to stick a needle in his neck and have him leave it in for an extended period of time. He refused and said he wanted to fly to Los Angeles for treatment by famed sports doctor Joe Kerlan. Nagashima made a negative remark about Davey's manhood during the incident, but Johnson flew to LA and Kerlan made quick work of solving the thumb problem. But there was a two-week delay in getting a return visa, which further strained his relationship with the Giants.

When he did return to Japan , Davey and the famed manager had a heart-to-heart and Johnson got across the point that he would be more productive "if you quit messing with me." Healthy again and able to strike out without being benched, Davey produced in the last half of the season and even blasted a "sayanora" (read: walk-off) homerun to clinch the league championship for the Giants.

Davey returned for a second season and became much more comfortable with life in the Japan. He bought an ultra luxury Toyota Century – sold only in Japan – and excelled for the Giants to the point that he hit 25 homers. "I enjoyed it. Japan is a great place," he says in retrospect. "I enjoyed my career, playing and managing in so many places and accomplishing what I did in so many of those places."

ONE OF HIS notable accomplishments as a player was to be the last man to get a hit off Dodgers' great Sandy Koufax. It came in the 1966 World Series in which Davey's Baltimore Orioles swept the Dodgers in four straight. Koufax was lifted after Davey's single in the seventh inning of the only game Koufax pitched in that Series. A few weeks later, Koufax surprised many by announcing his retirement at the age of just 30.

However, Koufax attended Dodgers' spring training in Vero Beach prior to the next season as a pitching instructor. That spring, Davey bumped into Koufax, who kidded him with: "You got that hit off of me. That's why I retired."

With the Orioles, Johnson was the starting second-baseman when the Orioles won four American League pennants and two World Series titles. He made four All-Star Game appearances while with Baltimore.

In 1973, after being traded to the Atlanta Braves, Johnson hit 43 home runs, more than any other second-baseman in Major League history and one more than the great Rogers Hornsby. Davey said he regaled at tying a player of Hornsby's stature, but was baffled that baseball officials later declared that one of Davey's homers that season was as a pinch-hitter, thus he remains "officially" tied with Hornsby.

The next season, there was an odd exchange with colorful Chicago Cubs manager Leo Durocher during the pregame . "You won't hit 20 homers this season, Leo sneered, implying that the 43 was a fluke. His dander up, Johnson countered: "Yeah? Well, you'll be lucky to be in baseball next year."

The feisty Durocher, piqued by Johnson's retort, had his pitcher deck Davey in the game that day. Johnson managed to duck the intended bean ball, but took a hard shot to his shoulder. A deep bruise from the pitch lingered much of that season, limiting his power. He lost the homerun derby by two to Willie Stargell of the Pirates.

THOSE ACCOMPLISHMENTS multiplied when he ended his playing career after two more seasons post-Japan, and launched a successful, albeit tumultuous 17 seasons as a field manager for the Mets, Reds, Orioles, Dodgers and Nationals – in addition to three minor-league clubs. He won at every level, including the short-lived InterAmerican League, an independent, roughly Triple-A league with teams in Miami and several Central and South American datelines. When the league folded 72 games into its first and only season, Johnson had guided the Miami team atop the standings with a 15-game lead. One thing he fondly remembers about that team was that Wendy's hamburger chain was one of the team's sponsors and a squad of vivacious base-sweeping girls -- named after the Wendy's slogan -- added some glitz to home games. "They were known," Davey recalls with a grin, "as the Hot-and-Juicy Girls."

Johnson earned the rare distinction of being named Manager of the Year in both the American and National Leagues – with ironic and amusing twists. He routinely clashed with his bosses – particularly GM Frank Cashen in New York, owner Marge Schott in Cincinnati and owner Peter Angelos in Baltimore.

Cashen, by many accounts, was jealous that Davey got most of the media credit for the Mets' successes and fired him after the 1990 season. Schott, a real-life cartoon character, openly criticized Davey and his fiancé Susan for briefly living together in Cincy before they were married and often angered Davey by sending "helpful" messages to him in the dugout during games. Angelos became miffed that strong-willed Davey made managerial decisions without input from the owner, who pushed him out.

Long after Johnson led the Mets to a World Series title, he and Cashen were inducted, somewhat awkwardly, into the Mets' Hall of Fame in the same ceremony. On the very day that Angelos pushed Johnson into resigning as Orioles' manager following the 1997 season, Davey was announced as AL Manager of the Year for leading the birds to back-to-back playoff appearances – their first in 13 years.

Davey clashed with Angelos, who didn't like that Johnson hadn't consulted him about the handling of an ugly incident in which infielder Sandy Alomar spit on an umpire. Davey fined Alomar and felt he had gotten the problem smoothed out. Angelos threatened to rescind the fine, but Davey explained that the Orioles would never get another close call from the umps if Alomar got off unpunished. Angelos recanted, but made up his mind to fire Johnson at the end of the season.

In Cincinnati, it was bad enough that owner Marge Schott made negative public comments about Susan, but Davey became further miffed that Marge fell into the habit of sending mid-game managerial suggestions to Davey in the dugout. The memos were always signed "Schottzie," Marge's ever-present pooch, and included paw prints. Obviously, the notes were from Marge and Davey sadly recalls one that was particularly offensive during a game in which the Reds were trailing: "You gonna pull this one out? If not, Susan won't go home with you tonight."

Marge didn't fire Davey right away, but did something more demeaning. She named former third-baseman Ray Knight as "co-manager" and made it clear Knight would be the team's manager the next season. "I like Ray, but that was a tough situation," Johnson recalls.

JOHNSON LIVES in Winter Park, Florida, where he made a name for himself as a youth baseball star. But he is far from retired. He joined the realty firm of Winter Park Land Company, which was founded 100 years ago by his grandfather, H.A. Ward. At 74, Davey is vice-president of the firm's commercial division.

He laments that so many in baseball have no active life after leaving the game. "So many guys get out of the game and feel their life is over," Davey sighed. "Two guys who were on my staff even committed suicide."

Chapter 14 -- Arnold Palmer, Greg Norman

In his heyday, Arnold Palmer was one of the global champions of golf. And drinking. This is not to suggest Arnie had a drinking problem. You try to keep up with Arnie in after-hours adult beverages and you lapse into semi-consciousness while wondering why Arnie is over there laughing at you. No problem.

He grew up in the hard-scrabble Western Pennsylvania steel-mill culture. The men of that time and place came to regard shots-and-beer as a standard refreshment not much different from the way the rest of us might regard lemonade or ginger ale. Thus, it was not uncommon throughout the 70's and 80's that at Arnie's Bay Hill Club in Orlando, or at the Latrobe Country Club where he grew up and eventually became the proprietor, that a shots-and-beer contest occasionally broke out after 18 holes of golf.

It would usually start with Arnie shaming friends into having a shot of whiskey followed by a glass of beer with him in the 19th hole. To affirm your manhood there before the King, you accepted. Then someone else would buy a second round and the game was on – Arnie knowingly leering at what he knew would take place. Then came another round, and another, while the room began to lose focus as you wondered when Arnie, noticeably unaffected by the powerful libations, grew a cast-iron stomach.

The capper of these contests to see who would be the last man standing happened during a Bay Hill Member-Guest tournament in the early '70s. It was Arnie against a field of five, all fully dressed in their golf attire. The five went in as 3-touchdown underdogs.

There appeared on the locker-room bar a row of six oversized shot glasses filled with whiskey and six beakers of beer. Each man stepped up to take his turn at bat. A joke or story would be shared as the containers were refilled for Round Two. One by one the pretenders began dropping out (*literally*, in some cases) while Arnie playfully chided the defectors. When only three remained, it should have been no surprise that all three had grown up in Latrobe pubs – insurance executive Danny Bonar, Latrobe foundry owner Chris Adams and the Living Legend, himself.

Bonar flamed out somewhere about round six and was carted off to former PGA champion Dow Finsterwald's nearby condo, where sketchy reports had it that Danny lost his cookies on one of Dow's flowered sofas. "Not so," Bonar later protested. An upbeat sort, Danny would alternately laugh and shake his head submissively at each retelling of the Great Shots and Beer Death Match.

Confirmed reports had it that Adams, a large man capable of handling his drink, went out on round eight in dramatic fashion. When he tilted his head back to throw down the whiskey and Rolling Rock beer (also a Latrobe staple), Adams never returned his head to the upright and locked position. He keeled over backward, his fall softened by a couple of spectators.

Arnie laughed, threw down his own No. 8 to seal the triumph, then dragged Adams into the showers, both fully clothed.

An hour later, Arnie delivered a brief welcoming address at the Member-Guest dinner with nary a slurred word or the slightest wobble.

GREG NORMAN, the dashing Australian, joined the impressive stable of PGA Tour pros based at Bay Hill in the early '80s. The storied daily "Shoot-out" competition was made up of amateur members divided into teams each typically captained by some Tour pro who resided in Central Florida. On any day, those captains might include the King himself, Arnold Palmer, Norman, Dow Finsterwald, AndyBean, Corey Pavin, Nick Price, Scott Hoch,

Payne Stewart or Mark O'Meara. Watching from the pro shop porch as the famed pros gathered on the first tee one day, longtime beloved Bay Hill club pro Richard Tiddy observed: "The Milwaukee Open would kill for this field!"

It was following one of those Shoot-outs that the Great White Shark was harpooned in one of Arnie's infamous shots-and-beer contests. Norman was more of a casual wine-with-dinner drinker, plus after-round beers. It is well known that Australians are required by law to consume at least a couple of Foster's after golf, tennis, rugby or whatever the exertion. But Norman was not thoroughly acclimated to hard liquor. Until that afternoon.

He was too proud to back down from Arnie's challenge, a regrettable decision. He recalled the post-mortems thusly:

"It took all the concentration I could muster to put one foot ahead of the other from the locker room to the parking lot and flop down in my little red Ferrari. I lived about four blocks from the clubhouse at that time." He somehow managed to avoid doing a "Tiger," navigating those four blocks without crashing into any fireplugs or mailboxes.

"But in concentrating on getting my feet to work, I had forgotten to take off my golf spikes," Norman recalled. "When I stepped out onto the concrete floor of my garage, the spikes shot out from under me and I fell flat on my back."

Greg's first wife, Laura, heard the commotion and threw open the door to discover her Greg, suave and dashing international golf star, lying on his back looking up at the slow-turning ceiling fan and laughing his head off. Repulsed that hubby was obviously drunk, she turned and stalked back into the house, leaving Greg on the concrete.

"Boy, did my head hurt the next morning," Greg remembers.

YOURS TRULY also became a victim of Arnie's shots-and-beer gambit. Knowing the long odds of remaining vertical if one foolishly accepts the challenge of trying to match Arnie drink-for-drink, I begged off several times before he insisted I prove my worth. I reluctantly agreed to have "just one" but he quickly poured another. For me, it only took about three of these deadly Western Pennsylvania boilermakers. They went down as if they were half whiskey and half molten lava. Your eyes water and in a few moments the worse seems to be over. You get goaded into a second round and your whole system starts dissolving in slow motion. The room begins swerving as if on a Daytona high-banked curve as you desperately cling to a chair back. Your tongue becomes silly putty and you wonder why Arnie is sitting there laughing instead of calling for a gurney.

In a spate of ill timing, this came only an hour or so before my wife and I were scheduled to share dinner with close friends -- Bay Hill member Paul Polizzi and his wife, Norma. By the time I somehow made it home, showered and dressed for dinner, I had lapsed into a state that might be called vertical comatose. I could see and hear. And I could walk – barely – but I couldn't talk. Over dinner in the club's elegant dining room, I was a zombie, an unblinking, muted mannequin.

When my tongue returned to normal a day or so later, I apologized profusely to the Polizzis. Paul just laughed. He had witnessed enough shots-and-beer victims in the Bay Hill locker room to understand my condition. My wife was not as understanding. She forgave me some time later – about three years later, as I recall.

ARNIE INVITED me to fly with him in his executive jet on several occasions. We shared social dinners and other events. We visited in one another's homes. I even caddied for him in the Houston Open on a golf magazine assignment in 90-degree heat. Thankfully, the tournament was cut to 54 holes after one round was rained out. We went to the clubhouse for lunch during the rainout, but a young lady at the door stopped Arnie in his tracks because he wasn't displaying the proper credentials to access the clubhouse dining room. She pointed to my caddy badge and said he needed something like that to get in.

"It's okay," I told her. "This old guy is with me."

Arnie's bubble-gum face variously contorted in indignation and amusement, obviously nonplussed that he needed affirmation from a lowly caddy-sportswriter, and that the woman hadn't recognized the global king of golf.

But the greatest humiliation might have been the day I bettered him in a social round of golf at Bay Hill. I was scheduled to fly out of Orlando that Friday afternoon to cover a Florida-Mississippi State football game that weekend in Mississippi. Arnie sent word he wanted to see me about doing a hole-by-hole pamphlet to be sold in the Bay Hill pro shop. When I stopped by en route to the airport, he said we could discuss the little project while playing in that day's Shootout. He had his secretary take my airline ticket and reschedule me on a later flight.

During the round, Arnie was trying out several drivers and shot an untidy 77. I was a high, single-digit handicap golfer at the time and had a career day with a 75. In all, we must have played golf 25 times and, if so, this raised my head-to-head record against him to 1-24. Within minutes I rushed to the airport and impersonated one of those old O.J. Simpson Hertz commercials, darting through the terminal leaping over luggage to make my flight. I boarded just as the door was closing and plopped down in my seat, exhausted and sweating, next to a well-dressed businessman.

I pulled out the seatback magazine, which opened, as fate would have it, right to a full-page ad of Arnie touting Lanier tape recorders. My first instinct was to point to the image and excitedly blurt to my seat-mate, "Hey, I just beat this guy by two strokes!"

Nahhhh. I wisely resisted. But I have always wondered what his skeptical reply might have been. Maybe: "And Winnie served you home-made cookies at the turn, right?"

ARNIE WAS and still is perhaps the most compelling sports figure in modern history. His blue-collar background and swashbuckling, go-for-broke style of play combined to produce a magnetic attraction from the sporting public. That relationship was refined and still endures well into his 80s because of the gracious style he extended to every member of what came to be known as Arnie's Army – fans, sponsors, tournament officials, volunteers and media. Every PGA Tour rookie should have been required to spend a couple of days paired with Arnie to absorb how you are supposed to treat the customers. One of those rookies, Eldridge Tiger Woods, was offered a valuable primer when Arnie invited him to lunch at Bay Hill. Concerned about how Tiger was imperiously conducting himself during the early part of his first year as a pro, Arnie urged him not to wait until the last minute to commit to his next tournament appearance, but rather commit early to allow that tournament to market their tickets and sponsorships. Arnie tried to tell him a softer touch with fans, volunteers and media would pay dividends over time.

The next day, I asked Arnie how much of his advice was taken to heart by Tiger, judging from the rookie's body language and responses. Arnie laughed and held up one hand, his thumb and forefinger arranged in a zero.

From my view, one of Arnie's few shortcomings was his habit of putting complete trust in his managers – the late Mark McCormack's powerful and murky International Management Group. Before the firm was sold to more trustworthy owners, IMG had a habit of double-dealing their own clients, including the shining star of their stable – Arnold Daniel Palmer. They often kept Arnie in the dark about finances and dealings that turned sour. Prime among those was Isleworth Country Club, a posh development just about a 3-wood from Bay Hill. It was to be the crowning benchmark of Palmer's course-design ventures and where he and Winnie would live out their golden years in a manse overlooking the idyllic Butler chain of lakes. Arnie partnered on the project with a Texas outfit, Concord Corporation, owned by a wealthy Mexican family.

But IMG chose to keep from Arnie the growing problem of an environmental no-no when drainage on two holes was surreptitiously diverted to Lake Bessie, a pristine 75-acre landlocked body of water along one side of the course. Approved engineering plans for Isleworth called for all drainage to flow into the Butler chain, which could better absorb and defuse the runoff. But shortly after the course opened, it was discovered that ugly black sludge from an unapproved, 42-inch drain pipe was fouling Lake Bessie and raising its level to the point it was destroying the docks, trees and shrubs of the charming, old-Florida homes on the opposite bank. Those longtime residents filed suit, but offered to settle for a mere $50,000 -- enough to simply plug the pipe and clean the lake.

IMG and their Orlando attorney haughtily told the residents to go pound sand. They tried to intimidate the residents into thinking they would be financially ruined in a counter-suit. Arnie got wind that something was amiss, but his IMG managers assured him there was no cause for concern and they were handling this "minor" situation. One of those residents, respected land attorney John Robertson, requested a meeting with Arnie to discuss the matter. He was denied. If that had happened, true friends of Arnie's suggested he and Robertson would have amicably resolved the problem and then retired to the bar to share a beer and laughs.

Instead, Robertson and his neighbors hired an engineer to keep gathering environmental evidence and raised the settlement offer slightly to cover their costs. The final offer was plug the pipe and $250,000. IMG kept telling them to go pound sand. Still no meeting with Arnie.

The case went to court, which ruled in the residents' favor and awarded them $6.6 million. The judgement sent the whole project into receivership, scuttling the Palmer-Concord venture and eventually leading to English financier Joe Lewis's purchase of Isleworth from Mellon Bank.

IMG was also less than candid with Arnie when they pushed him to sell Bay Hill Club and Lodge to a Japanese group. He had little interest in selling, but IMG kept wearing him down with the alleged offer price of $48 million. The group put up a $3 million deposit and the story broke. Even Winnie Palmer was livid at the notion of her All-American husband selling Bay Hill to some Japanese group."This is like John Wayne selling the prairie to Japan," someone tersely observed. But the deal collapsed when the buyers cited underground chemical tanks that IMG had "forgotten" to disclose.

One wonders why Arnie kept trusting his former IMG managers in the face of such PR and monetary double bogeys. Stars such as Nicklaus, Norman, Wadkins and Crenshaw had dumped IMG as their managers. One evening in the Bay Hill locker room, after a round of drinks, one of Arnie's truest friends – a major Charlotte businessman -- advised: "You need to get away from IMG. They can soil even your image."

Arnie's alleged reply: "Listen, they put $25 million on my hip each year. What do I care if they steal two or three."

MY CHUMMY relationship with Arnie turned chilly with the publishing of my 1993 book, *"Arnie: Inside the Legend."* Not because of what was in it, but rather what IMG *told* Arnie would be in it. Parts of this chapter were referenced in that book. But there have been no public revelations about what Arnie did when his agents convinced him the book would include one chapter alleging many infidelities and another covering his daughter Amy's breast cancer – a delicate, off-limits subject to the Palmers at the time.

No such chapters existed, but IMG was eager to make Arnie mad at me and hoped to scuttle the book because they could tell from my sticky questions during lengthy interviews with McCormack and his top aide,

Alastair Johnston, that IMG was going to be roughed up in the book. Alas, Arnie embraced their lies.

Several years earlier, Arnie had assured me I could co-author his biography. Then I discovered that IMG had engaged their own author to do the work, cutting out yet another interloper (me) who had gotten too close to Palmer for their comfort. When I told Arnie what I had learned, I said I was going to go ahead and write the book on my own and hoped he would cooperate with it. He did. He sat for several long interviews to flesh out some of the details of anecdotes and allowed me to borrow and copy several private framed photographs in his Bay Hill home to use in my book.

But when IMG falsely convinced him of the impending trumped-up chapters, Arnie intercepted me one day in the Bay Hill parking lot. It was on the very day that the book was first being printed. He twisted his face into a dark scowl and issued this stern edict that I can clearly hear to this day: "You'd better be careful what is in your book. I have friends in Korea who said they will do *anything* for me. *Anything!* You understand?"

I very clearly understood the implications and had been around him for enough years to know he wasn't joking. I didn't really think he would put out a contract on me; I figured he was just trying to intimidate me into a last-minute rewrite if what his agents had told him was true. But I didn't want to take any chances.

I reported the threat to my *Orlando Sentinel* editor, John Haile. In case my body was to wash up on Lake Butler, I thought it would be helpful to the police to know who the first person of interest they might want to interrogate. Haile called Arnie to express his concern. Arnie invited him to Bay Hill and, over lunch, insisted his comment was only a joke.

Ha-ha. What a jokester, that Arnold Palmer.

The book was barely on the shelves when Arnie told a national golf magazine I had no scruples. IMG fanned the flames by mounting a campaign to discredit me, the book and warn booksellers they might be included as defendants if IMG sued me. (I knew that wasn't going to happen because I had several of their transgressions documented, and because the last thing they wanted was for me to go through their files during the discovery phase of a trial.) The book was introduced at a New Jersey media hotel function two days before the 1993 U.S. Open at Baltusrol Golf Club. IMG dispatched one of their minions to pick up a copy and overnight it directly to IMG headquarters in Cleveland.

When they read the chapter titled "Darth McCormack and the Evil Empire," McCormack and Johnston penned a dark internal memo detailing an underhanded game plan for damaging sales of the book. That very day, an IMG employee who was uncomfortable with the firm's dark tactics, faxed a copy of the memo to me at that New Jersey hotel.

The book drew overwhelmingly positive reviews and many Tour principals had trouble understanding Arnie's ire at a book that, on balance, polished his star even more. IMG's discomfort was obvious: (1) some of their lowly deeds had been exposed in the book and (2) they weren't making a dime off of a book about their No. 1 client.

Their first act of retribution by IMG was to order the Bay Hill Club general manager to triple my slightly discounted membership dues. I was disappointed that Arnie, once again, stood by and allowed IMG to make his decisions. But several other significant clubs in the Orlando area shook their heads at the unseemly move and offered me a membership at whatever my Bay Hill discounted dues had been.

One pro famously quoted a locker-room comment by Tour star Tom Kite: "What's Arnie upset about? Larry's book makes you love Arnie more and IMG less. And that's the way it should be." (It must be noted here that McCormack, at the urging of his wife, former tennis star Betsey Nagelson, became a born-again Christian and softened his tactics a bit. Months after his death in 2003, IMG was sold to a coalition of William Morris Endeaver and Silver Lake Partners. By all accounts, the new owners have significantly raised the integrity image of the firm.)

Several weeks after the book's release, Arnie saw to it that I was invited to a cocktail party in the main Bay Hill Club bar. I pulled on a bulletproof vest (just kidding) and attended. At one point, Arnie approached me away from the small crowd and said, "Some of my friends tell me your book was actually pretty good." He shook my hand and added: "We're still friends, right?"

Nope. I had tooted his horn for 20 years in many of my newspaper columns and then wrote a book about what a swell guy he is. Then he chose to believe his IMG agents about the content and threatened me. Friends don't treat friends like that. I said a professional relationship would be more appropriate. His face twisted through assorted expressions as it was his turn to see if I was kidding. I wasn't.

During the remaining several years before I retired from the *Sentinel,* he routinely returned my phone calls if there was a developing story about him or his tournament. Even after he was diagnosed with prostate cancer, underwent surgery in Minnesota and imposed a temporary media blackout, I was the first one he allowed to interview him about the ordeal.

But the plane rides, the socializing and the golf matches were history. Maybe he was afraid I might raise my record against him to 2-24?

Despite his few flaws – and we all have them – I still think Arnold Palmer is a highly commendable and caring person who raised a sport to new and unthinkable heights. And if you think he's not funny, then you never had the pleasure of hearing him walk up and down the aisle of his Citation jet, singing the punch line to a shaggy dog joke – "I left my haaaaarp, in Sam Frank's discooooooooo....."

BACK TO GREG NORMAN. I had the pleasure of playing a number of rounds of social golf with the Shark and mutual friends, usually at Bay Hill or Grand Cypress resort, where Greg had an affiliation with that club's preeminent golf instructor, Fred Griffin.

One day the match at Grand Cypress was Greg and Jim English, co-owner of United Health Care which owned several hospitals, against me and fellow amateur Ron Larimer, a successful local businessman. We were playing a golf betting game called "Vegas," in which each team's score was reversed if neither player made par or better. Thus, if Ron made par 4 and I made 5, our team score was 45. If Greg and his partner made birdie 3 and par 4, their score was 34. Thus, they win by 11, or $11 on this one hole in our dollar-a-point match.

Greg was hot that day and he and English were already killing us before disaster struck on the seventh hole, a dogleg right around a lake. Ron pushed his drive into the water, then dropped a ball and tried a long, risky shot over the lake to the green. He was just short, plunking it into the lake again. He had to hit again from the same spot, now playing his fifth shot. Obviously, he was going to make a high number and our scores would be reversed if I failed to make par. I made bogey 5. Ron suffered a nine. That meant our score was 95 to Greg and his partner's 44. My Mississippi math made it apparent they had just beaten us by 51 points, or $51 dollars on a single hole. For a guy on a sportswriter's salary, this was a rocket-propelled grenade right to the chest.

This match came only a couple of weeks after Greg had seen yet another major victory yanked away when Bob Tway, a spindly, curly-haired Oklahoma pro, holed out a miracle bunker shot on the 72nd hole at Inverness to nip Norman for the 1986 PGA Championship. That was deadly serious. Our social matches in Orlando were not. We were fun-loving, raucous friends and no joke or jab was off limits. Almost.

A few holes after the $51 disaster, we took on a par 5 with a water hazard running along the right side of the fairway. Long drivers could gamble and cut part of the lake, rewarding themselves with a chance to reach the green in two. As Greg addressed the ball, I muttered just loud enough for Greg to hear: "Bob Tway….Bob Tway….Bob Tway…"

The other two players jolted in shock and covered their faces to hide their grins as Norman stiffened in extra concentration. He unleashed a furious swing to cut off part of the lake, but the ball drifted too far to the right and into the water.

Now the other bad news. Greg and I were riding together. He returned to the cart stone-faced and didn't say another word to me the remainder of the round. Greg made bogey on the hole and Ron and I trimmed two dollars off of our growing deficit. Ron was afraid to get too close to me, no doubt fearing he might become collateral damage if Greg attacked me with a sand wedge.

But no attack and no words until we were through and entered the clubhouse to freshen up. Then Greg turned to me with a broad smile. "That was a shitty thing to do, you s.o.b." he chortled and broke out laughing. "Let's get a beer."

Fortunately, Greg picked up the tab and I think Ron subsidized most of my golf losses that day. That was only just. *He* was the one who made 9 on that disastrous hole. I was the one who made the over-the-top gaff. And Greg was the one who proved he could be a good sport, even under trying circumstances.

Chapter 15 – Hawk Harrelson

KEN "Hawk" HARRELSON came out of Savannah, Georgia, a large multi-sport athlete loaded with talent and self-confidence. After starring in several sports in high school, Hawk chose to concentrate on baseball. A power hitter with few peers, he became a flamboyant, popular and sometimes controversial, outspoken superstar, whose 9-year major-league career peaked in 1968 when he was an All-Star and led the American League in runs batted in for the Boston Red Sox. He followed that with 30 homers in a 1969 season split between the Red Sox and Cleveland Indians. He has spent the past 30 seasons as the lead broadcaster for Chicago White Sox games, drawing accolades (5 Emmys) and criticism for being a cheerleading "homer" on-air for the White Sox, an assertion he welcomes.

That adversarial relationship with the Chicago media reached a zenith in 1968 when Hawk came out from behind the mike to spend one season as general manager of the White Sox. The press took delight in second-guessing Hawk's GM moves, especially when he fired manager Tony La Russa after the team got off to a dreadful, 26-38 start. "I called Tony in and said I had to make him a hero or fire him," Hawk recalls. "Tony said I couldn't make him a hero, so that settled it."

La Russa recovered to win three World Series and 12 division championships mostly as skipper of the Oakland A's and St. Louis Cardinals. His teams won more than 2,700 games, putting him behind only managerial legends Connie Mack and John McGraw, and was inducted into baseball's Hall.

La Russa and the gregarious Harrelson remain good friends to this day. At a charity golf tournament in St. Louis that Tony organized to fund one of the several charities he supports, Harrelson put on a long-drive clinic and entertained the crowd with quips and stories from his madcap career. "Tony managed for 33 years and was fired only once," he told them. "And I was the asshole who did it."

Engagingly outgoing, the fun-loving slugger collected almost as many hilarious memories as home runs (131) during his injury-shortened baseball career. Then he turned to golf and tried to make it as a tour pro, but showed more promise than results. Thankfully, he had the gift of being able to laugh at his own foibles.

The first of those came in his rookie season with Kansas City in a spring training game in Fort Lauderdale against the vaunted New York Yankees. Hawk was playing first base "while just a kid," he recounts.

Leadoff hitter Bobby Richardson "hit a shin-burner that bounced off my knee." One error.

Next up, Joe Pepitone, who "just scorches one. It takes a hop and hits me in the left shoulder." Two errors.

"Finally, Elston Howard comes up and hits a rocket right down the third-base line that I knew was headed for the left-field corner. I'm just watching. But, somehow, Ed Charles, our third-baseman, dives to the right, made the play, wheeled and made a perfect throw right over the (first-base) bag. And I'm just standing there about 20 feet away, watching it."

Like it was yesterday, Hawk recalled that Yankee legends Yogi Berra and Joe DiMaggio were sitting in chairs near the fence, not far from first base. "They were laughing their butts off. The first-base umpire -- I think it was Nestor Chylak -- said, 'Hawk, don't stop now. I think you've got 'em right where you want 'em!'

"That was funny and embarrassing. I made two errors of commission and one error of omission in the span of about six minutes."

Welcome to the Big Leagues.

HAWK OVERCAME that humbling start to become a feared power hitter, but there were plenty of other red-faced moments to come.

He and fellow Red Sox star Carl Yastrzemski went for a late-night dinner after a game in Cleveland to a place called Theatrical, where a lot of players frequented because it stayed open late and the guys could have a nice dinner there even after night games.

"There were not many people in the place that particular night," Hawk recalls. "Yaz and I ordered steaks and a beer, and I noticed a big guy sitting in the back of the dining room. In about 30 minutes, here comes the big guy I had noticed." It turned out to be Sam McDowell – Sudden Sam – the ace of the Cleveland staff, who was scheduled to start against Hawk and the Red Sox the next night.

"Sam didn't even look at Yaz, but he looked me in the eye and said, 'Hawk, I'm going to blow your ass away four times tomorrow night, on nothing but fastballs.' "

I said, 'Get out of here Sam. I don't need any of your BS.' "

First time up, Sam started with a fastball and Hawk connected, hitting it all the way out of mammoth, old Cleveland Municipal Stadium. But about 15 feet foul.

"He never threw me another fastball that night. I kept looking for the fast ball and he'd throw me a curve. I'd look for a fastball and here came a slider. I'd look for the fastball and he'd throw a changeup. He struck me out four times. Obviously, he was just conning me the night before in the restaurant. I was the dummy."

HAWK HAD his biggest game in Cleveland under some unusual circumstances.

A couple of guys he knew, Larry Mako and Scott Reed, set him up the night before Hawk would be facing the great Luis Tiant in a day game. Tiant was in his prime and virtually unhittable. Hawk's "pals" took him out to a place called The Blue Grass – a cabaret – where they partied too late and didn't allow Hawk much sleep to recoup.

In recalling the incident for this book, Hawk was reluctant to say why he was in a fog the next day. He wanted to dance around some details that he wouldn't want any of his "kids and grandkids" to read. Let's just say he had too many blueberry milkshakes that night. "Suffice it to say I was hurting," he grinned.

"Luis was throwing nearly 100 miles per hour and with every pitch I was seeing three balls. He got me the first time up, but in my next at-bat, somehow, my bat found the right ball and I hit it over the centerfield fence, 440 feet for a home run. I was the most surprised guy in the ball park. I wound up hitting two more homers that day, driving in all seven of our runs as we won, 7-2."

Hawk later found out that his two "friends" had made a large wager on Cleveland for that game and decided they could assure winning the bet by neutralizing Hawk. "They knew I was the only one on our team swinging the bat well at that time. Afterward, they apologized and promised they'd never do that again. I wasn't very happy because I never bet on a game in my life."

Hawk couldn't stay too mad, however, as his manager, Dick Williams, made the decision that night to include him in his All-Star Game lineup that summer.

For a game in Baltimore, when he was with Kansas City, Hawk had a little vision trouble again. Let's just say he caught hay fever in some smoky, late-night establishment and his eyes were watering. This time he was seeing "only" two balls, but he picked out the right one to blast another tape-measure homer.

While playing baseball, Hawk continued to develop his promising golf game between seasons. When he retired from baseball in midseason, 1971, due to an injury, he turned pro and took a shot at playing the PGA Tour.

"That's when I learned to write checks instead of cashing them," Hawk laments, adding with a laugh, "I have $220,000 in canceled checks to prove I can't play tour golf."

He got into a number of PGA Tour events on sponsor exemptions, but his highlight was winning a couple of pre-tournament long-driving contests against some of the Tour pros. He made the cut in just one PGA Tour event for a couple thousand dollars and picked up some small change playing on sponsor exemptions on the European Tour. "I was getting calls from tournaments all over the world. Japan, Australia, you name it. They liked that I was a baseball player and could hit the ball so far. In Japan, they wanted to match me against the great Jumbo Ozaki in a driving contest."

In his brief forays on the PGA Tour, Hawk developed a friendship with Jack Nicklaus. They played a few practice rounds and as the 1972 British Open approached, Nicklaus said, "Hawk, you're playing too good not to go over and try to qualify for the British Open."

Sounded like fun to Hawk, so he sent in his entry. He was assigned to a 36-hole qualifier at Gullane Golf Club, which is the sister course to Muirfield, where the 1972 Open was being contested. Hawk led the first qualifying round with a 66 and finished the 36-hole qualifier second only to Bruce Devlin, who went on to become an established figure on the PGA Tour. Hawk shot 6-under and Devlin shot 7-under for the two days. Both made the field for the Open, which was to start in two days.

Back then, the British Open wasn't played on Sunday. First round was on Wednesday and the final on Saturday. Hawk played a Muirfield practice round on Tuesday with Nicklaus, Tom Weiskopf and Florida pro Bert

Yancey. Nicklaus had already won the first two majors that year, the Masters and the U.S. Open. Thus he had a shot to win all four majors that year – the elusive Grand Slam of golf.

"On the first hole, Jack said he was impressed with the way I had played in the qualifier. I looked at him and said. 'Jack, I realize you're trying to win the Slam. But I'm gonna try to win this s.o.b. myself."

Amused, Nicklaus responded: "Hawk, I'm glad. That's the way you should feel."

Hawk added, "I promise you one thing. I won't leave any putt short."

Indeed, Hawk charged every birdie putt. He shot 75 in the opening round, despite six three-putts. Still charging those birdie opportunities in the second round, he suffered five more three-putts. "I'd have a 20-foot putt and would leave an 8-footer coming back. I'd have a 10-footer and leave a six-footer coming back. I had eleven three-putts in the first two rounds and missed the cut by only one shot. Tee to green, nobody hit the ball better that week than I did."

He had the Scottish fans in awe with his long-distance clouts. In the two rounds at Gullane, two practice rounds at Muirfield and two rounds in the tournament, Hawk never hit his driver in one of Muirfield's maddening fairway bunkers. "I was hitting the ball so far, I just carried all the bunkers. I didn't have any problem with them," he recalls.

However, that didn't apply to his approach shots to the green and one of those occasions proved to be an educational and shocking experience for the British Open rookie. Flamboyant pro Doug Sanders recommended a Scottish caddy who was a banker in real life. Hawk discovered that lots of Scottish businessmen back then took time off during the Open week to caddy for some of the competitors.

"What I didn't realize was that they think of the player and caddy as a team and expect all decisions to be made jointly," says Hawk. "He drove me around, picked me up at the hotel and so forth. He was like my valet off the course.

"We already had a couple of differences on club selection when we came to an approach shot to a par-4 hole. He said it called for an eight-iron. I said, 'Nah, I like the nine.' He insisted I should use the eight, but I told him I was going to hit the nine."

"I hit the nine right on line with the flag. But it was a few feet short and buried into the face of the bunker guarding the green. We could see the ball stuck in the lip of the bunker. I had no shot." Had he taken the caddy's advice, he presumably would have safely reached the green.

With that, the caddy took Hawk's bag off his shoulder, put it on the ground and walked off without a word. Hawk called after him, asking, "Don't you want your money?' But he didn't even respond. Just kept walking. The people at the club got another caddy for me."

SOMETHING SIMILAR happened when Hawk decided to play a few events on the European Tour to get some pro tournament seasoning. He took his own caddy, an Italian-American friend named Joe Nunnari. "We called him Joe Namath because he looked a lot like Namath. He was to be my caddy in Spain at the Madrid Open. But being of Italian descent, he wanted to first make a visit to Rome. So I gave him some extra money to go to Rome and meet me back at the Madrid airport when I arrived."

At the airport, Hawk could tell Joe "Namath" obviously had gotten into some Rome food or drink that didn't agree with him. When they reached the golf course for a practice round, the caddy began turning various colors. Then Joe began throwing up and had to be replaced. There was a vacationing American from Chicago in the gallery, who turned out to be a lawyer for the White Sox. He filled in until Joe could get up off of his all fours."

"By the end of the tournament, Joe had recovered and we went to the Spanish Open up near the French border. I played a practice round with Jack Newton, the promising Australian who later lost an arm when he walked into an airplane propeller.

"The wind was blowing so hard, I asked an official with the R&A if they were going to cancel the round. He just shook his head. They were having what they call 'force nine' winds – roughly 60 mph. There were players out on the practice tee practicing topping 2-irons just to be sure they could advance the ball against such fierce winds.

"So we get out on the course and something happened I've never heard about being done," Hawk recalled. "On a tee shot into that wind, I was blown off the ball a little on my downswing and I hit a solid, but very high drive." A major-league popup. Hawk watched in disbelief as the ball began drifting back toward him and came down about 15 yards *behind* the tee. *Behind the tee!*

"I've never heard of that before."

Playing downwind in such a gale was a different matter. "The very next hole was a par-5 that was nearly 600 yards," Hawk continued. "Now we are going downwind and the fairways were hard. The ball would roll forever. I hit a big drive that carried far down the fairway and began rolling. It stopped about eight yards short of a greenside bunker."

Chapter 16 – Bob Baffert, Ernie Els, Jimmy Johnson, George Steinbrenner, Seve Ballesteros, Clint Hurdle

BOB BAFFERT, recent Triple Crown winning trainer of American Pharoah, has become a regular headliner at the thoroughbred classics after saddling his first Kentucky Derby entry in 1996. That would be Cavonnier, an impressive colt that ran second. Baffert would win the next two Derbys to kick start his dominance in the three classics – Kentucky Derby, Preakness and Belmont.

That first year at the Derby in Louisville, the jocular Baffert decided to get his trademark shock of coiffed white hair trimmed a couple days before the big race. Being California-cool, Bob had no interest in going to a conventional barbershop, so he asked around among the Churchill Downs executives for the name of an upscale styling shop in town. Given a recommendation, he phoned the salon to set up an appointment for the next day.

Being a discriminating shop, he was asked a few questions after he explained he was a Californian in town for the Kentucky Derby. They would look askance if Bob were some lowly groom or – heaven forbid -- one of the grimy workers who mucked out the stables.

"What is it that you do?" the lady stylist asked.

"I'm a porn movie star," he declared, tongue in cheek.

Without hesitation, the lady gave him an appointment time and apparently shared the exciting information with her co-workers. When he arrived the next day, he discovered that the stylists had aggressively argued over which of them would get to service a "porn star."

ERNIE ELS, a truly global golf star, typically includes appearances each year on a half-dozen different pro tours around the world. That's a lot of travel and a lot of different hotel and resort accommodations – usually high end. Thus was the case in 1994 when Ernie, the long-hitting South African with the nickname "The Big Easy," played the Doral Open in Miami and bedded down right there onsite in the venerable, but upscale Doral Resort.

Relaxing between rounds, Els was sprawled across the bed, face-down, reading a newspaper he had spread out on the carpet. "I heard this scratching sound that seemed to be coming from the closet," he recalls, making a clawing motion with the fingers on one hand. He cracked open the closet door and out scurried a large rat. Leizel, Ernie's wife, did what ladies are required by law to do at the sight of a mouse: She leaped up on the bed, squealing in fright.

In his easy-going nature, Ernie simply picked up the phone and called the front desk to report the uninvited guest in his room. The hotel dispatched its animal removal team and after a spirited chase, managed to catch and remove the rat.

At the end of the tournament, when Els checked out at the front desk, he reminded them of the critter. The clerk apologized profusely and made a magnanimous offer to appease the golf star. He discounted Ernie's thousand-dollar-plus bill by $50.

Now we know the going discount for a rodent in your Doral room in 1994: Fifty bucks.

Since then, the Doral Golf Resort was purchased and upgraded by flamboyant New York real estate mogul and presidential candidate

Donald Trump. No word as of this writing if The Donald has adjusted the price of mice.

GEORGE STEINBRENNER, the late bellicose and high-profile New York Yankees owner, became a friend when I covered his thoroughbred entries in the Kentucky Derby. As president of the FloridaThoroughbred Breeders Association, he even invited me to be the featured speaker at the FTBA annual meeting in Ocala one year.

A few weeks later, George was the speaker at a youth group meeting in Orlando. The engagement was on the same evening as that historic "No, Mas!" closed-circuit television fight between Sugar Ray Leonard and Roberto Duran. I called the promoter who was putting on the telecast at the Orlando Expo Center convention hall, and he was kind enough to provide three front-row seats for George, my wife Mary and me. We picked up George as his speaking engagement concluded and dashed over to the telecast just before the featured fight began.

In the folding chairs right behind us were three young Orlando bankers who had obviously spent most of the time during the prelim bouts pounding beers. They instantly recognized Steinbrenner and began showering him with provocative, sticky questions. Although known for his occasional eruptions, George endured the alcohol-fueled heckling and responded in a smiling, gentlemanly fashion.

A couple of rounds into the fight, we began to smell an overwhelmingly sweet, pungent odor. One of the bankers had upchucked and his vomit was flowing beneath our chairs and around our feet. The promoter was summoned and moved us to another location. The bankers, no doubt, were fearful that I might identify in the newspaper the bank they were so poorly representing. But I never did document they worked for SunTrust Bank and presumably were able to keep their jobs. Let's keep their embarrassment a secret just between us.

I witnessed the infamous darker side of Steinbrenner when I went to New York to cover a World Series between his Yankees and the Los Angeles Dodgers. On the day before the first game, I went to his Yankee Stadium office to say hello. He was gracious and asked if there was anything he could do for me while in New York.

In part because I was from a non-league city, I had been issued sort of a B-grade press credential that permitted access only to the interview room and not the field or locker rooms. George exploded. He called in his secretary and reminded her – in an R-rated discourse – that he had instructed her to tell team press director Marty Appel that he wanted full credentials issued to his friends in the Florida media. Then he called Appel on the carpet and ramped up the dark language – all in front of me.

I sought out Appel immediately afterward and apologized for what he had to endure. He shook his head and allowed as how that was the norm, working for George.

It was also the norm for those women unfortunate enough to hire on as George's secretary. I learned that each time a new one was hired, the team staff privately conducted a pool to guess what day the new girl would quit in tears or be fired.

I also learned of the softer side of Steinbrenner. On a flight, I happened to sit next to George's finance man, who became quite candid about The Boss. One particularly compelling story was the time George read in the Tampa paper about a hard-luck single mother who was struggling with the rent and about to lose her hair-styling business. That day, $10,000 appeared in her personal bank account and she never learned (unless she reads it here) that her benefactor was tough old George Steinbrenner.

SEVE BALLESTEROS was widely known in the public as a charismatic and fiercely competitive champion golfer who led and inspired the European Ryder Cup team to end the long-standing U.S. dominance. The handsome

Spaniard led the Euros to five Ryder Cup victories both as a player and captain before he tragically died of brain cancer at only 54.

Tour golf insiders, while fully appreciating Seve's greatness (5 major titles, 50 European Tour wins), were also aware that Seve practiced a high degree of gamesmanship on the course, using grey areas of the rules to discombobulate opponents and sometimes intimidate officials into a favorable ruling.

American Paul Azinger was one of his more celebrated victims when Seve hinted aloud that Paul was fudging the rules. Other pros with a higher degree of mental toughness were able to withstand Seve's tactics and one even managed to turn the tables.

Playing in a European Tour event while paired with Ballesteros, Zimbabwean pro Tony Johnstone, who won eight times on the Euro Tour, nimbly set a trap for Seve. The two had pulled their drives just off the left side of a fairway and over a small rise. Johnstone walked over the rise first and immediately took up a stance over a ball that was partially blocked by the trunk of a small tree a few yards ahead, but within a few feet of a sprinkler head. By rule, a player is allowed a free drop clear of a sprinkler head as long as one foot comes in contact with the sprinkler head when the player takes his *normal* stance. In this case, a drop would permit a player to move the ball two club lengths to one side and, thus clear of the tree trunk.

As Seve cleared the rise, Johnstone took an exaggerated open stance that allowed him to reach back with his left foot on the sprinkler head. "I can take a drop from the sprinkler, right?" he asked.

"No, no, no. No drop," countered the Spaniard.

Johnstone reversed to a drastically closed stance, allowing him to extend his right foot back to make contact with the sprinkler. "What about now?" he asked.

"No, no. No drop," Seve repeated.

"Good. Play it, then. This is YOUR ball," said Johnstone who walked a few yards away to his own ball.

In retelling the story, Johnstone laughed when revealing the outcome: "Seve curved it around the tree trunk and made par anyway, while I bogeyed the hole."

CLINT HURDLE, who has become an icon of late as manager of the resurgent Pittsburgh Pirates, was a heralded phenom when he first burst out of Merritt Island, Florida, and onto the cover of *Sports Illustrated*. After first committing to the University of Miami as a quarterback, he instead signed a baseball contract with the Kansas City Royals. He became a valued cog for the Royals as a power-hitting outfielder when the team won the American League pennant and faced Philadelphia in the 1980 World Series.

But not as valued as Hurdle desired.

During the last half of that season, manager Jim Frye relegated Hurdle to platoon duty, alternating in right field with Jose Cardenal. Clint was in the starting lineup against right-handed starters and Jose was in against lefties. Like all young players, Clint felt he could be more productive if he were in the lineup every day and repeatedly badgered Frye about it.

When the Royals reached the Series, I managed to talk Clint into doing a brief daily report in the *Orlando Sentinel* under a heading that included his photo and the headline, "Hey, Mom, I'm in the Series!" The arrangement called for me to talk to him each day, collect his behind-the-scenes pearls as the Series progressed and ghost-write a short "column" for Clint.

But he came up with the opening line on his own for the initial report: "I want to thank the *Sentinel* for allowing me to do these reports and, mainly, for committing to use them every day against left- and right-handed printers."

At a recent charity golf tournament that Clint hosted in his Florida hometown, I addressed the crowd and told them about that opening line. Hurdle blushed and laughed as he took the mike to say: "Can you imagine how I would react if one of my Pirates players came to me with such a demand?"

The daily Clint blurb provided a national scoop for me, though Clint would prefer I not relate the indelicate situation. At one point in that Series, Clint told me that Royals future Hall of Famer George Brett had come down with a severe case of hemorrhoids and might even have to (painfully) sit out the next game. I broke the story that night in the *Sentinel*, which was picked up immediately by the wire services. Brett wound up playing the next game but had to gingerly sit on an inflated donut cushion in the dugout between innings.

Hurdle was one of the first to become aware of Brett's problems because Clint had had the same problem earlier that year. "George made fun of me back then, kidding me about the ailment," Clint recalled. "But when *he* became the victim, he came running to me to frantically ask what I did for relief."

Then and now, Clint always looked up to Brett and especially appreciated the jocular tactic George used to calm young Hurdle at the outset of his first major-league game. The occasion was 1978 opening day at Cleveland's old, monstrous Memorial Stadium and players from both teams were introduced pre-game as they lined up along the first- and third-base foul lines.

"There were seventy-thousand people in that huge stadium and the noise was louder than I had ever heard. I already had the jitters, but as I stood there and heard my name announced, I could hardly breathe," Hurdle recalls.

Brett noticed his rookie teammate was overcome. He jabbed Clint and offered some playful encouragement. "Let's get five hits today," said

Brett. "I'll get four and you get one." Both laughed and Clint's breathing returned to normal.

We close this tome with a situation that would have been a perfect fit for *Reader's Digest's* once-popular feature called "The Perfect Squelch." When the Dallas Cowboys gave Miami Hurricanes coach JIMMY JOHNSON his chance to coach in the NFL in 1989, Johnson quickly accepted, then had a shocking pronouncement for his wife. Linda Kay Johnson is a delightfully engaging southern lady who was popular with other coaches and their wives in the coaching fraternity.

But after being lured by Jerry Jones to coach the Cowboys, whom Johnson would eventually lead to two Super Bowl titles in his five seasons in Dallas, Jimmy announced to Linda Kay that she would not be making the travel squad. Johnson privately admitted to close friends that he felt it necessary to project a "family" image as long as he was working at the collegiate level, where recruiting and a G-rated personal image are important. However, he didn't feel such a sunny marital aura was mandatory at the pro level.

In breaking the news to Linda Kay, Jimmy urged that it was his desire that their breakup be as congenial as possible and promised to provide anything she would need as a divorcee. Once she recovered from the unexpected shock and had a handle on her emotions, she noted that for starters she would need a car. In Jimmy's contract with the University of Miami, the school had provided two new automobiles each year, one for Jimmy and one for Linda Kay. Now those cars would have to be returned and Linda Kay would be without wheels.

Johnson readily agreed and instructed her to go pick out a car and send the invoice to Jimmy's secretary, who paid all of his personal bills. Given that Linda Kay was pleasingly unpretentious, Jimmy assumed she would pick out a nice garden-variety Chevy or Toyota, or something modestly similar in the $20,000 neighborhood.

She was peeved enough that she had another neighborhood in mind.

When the secretary presented Jimmy with the invoice, Linda Kay's new chariot turned out to be a head-turning, $84,000 foreign luxury sedan. She should have come to be known not as Linda Kay, but "Eighty-Four K."

Asked about it years later, Jimmy laughed and admitted: "Yep. She got me."

The End

ABOUT THE AUTHOR – After stints at the Brookhaven (Miss.) *Daily Leader* and Jackson (Miss.) *Clarion-Ledger*, **LARRY GUEST** moved to *The Orlando Sentinel* where he was the paper's syndicated lead sports columnist for 28 years until his retirement in 2000. He earned status as one of the nation's most respected and well-known sports columnists. Three times, he was voted by his peers the Sports Writer of the Year in Florida, a state blessed with a plethora of colorful and gifted sports scribes.

His graceful, witty style connected with readers. He dearly loved to often break local and national sports news stories, a penchant that inspired the late Payne Stewart to give his friend Guest the teasing nickname "Scoop." Those news breaks were spawned mostly by his ability to develop close, professional/social relationships with many of the sports headliners he covered– including many of the personalities featured in this, his seventh book.

Two of his previous books, "ARNIE: Inside the Legend" and "The Payne Stewart Story," made various best-seller lists. The other tomes were "Making Magic" an account of Orlando's acquisition of an NBA franchise with Magic exec Pat Williams, "Confessions of a Coach" with NCAA champion basketball coach Norm Sloan, "Larry Guest Lite," a collection of Guest's more humorous columns, and "Built To Win," with Atlanta Braves GM John Schuerholz. Most of those remain available at Amazon.com.

Guest and his wife Mary reside in Cape Canaveral, FL. Their three daughters have earned accolades in engineering, hospital finance and teaching. They have seven grandchildren.

To contact Guest or read more about his books and occasional blogs, visit www.larryguest.com

58246643R00087

Made in the USA
Charleston, SC
07 July 2016